DOGFISH MEMORY

DOGFISH MEMORY

SAILING IN SEARCH
OF OLD MAINE

JOSEPH DANE

THE COUNTRYMAN PRESS
WOODSTOCK, VERMONT

Design and composition by S. E. Livingston

Dogfish Memory
978-0-88150-955-7

Published by The Countryman Press,
P.O. Box 748, Woodstock, VT 05091

Distributed by W. W. Norton & Company, Inc.,
500 Fifth Avenue, New York, NY 10110

Printed in the United States of America

10 9 8 7 6 5 4 3 2 1

Für Elise

PREFACE

Change. Change is bad.

      —Linda Jane, mocking me

I have a lot of hippie friends, although now there are different names for them. They cut and split their firewood to heat the houses they have built themselves. They grow their own vegetables and on a good year they'll still be eating them in spring. Most grew up elsewhere. They range in age from twenty to eighty-five. All of us play Maine in our own ways, although I grow nothing more complex than rhubarb and I cannot operate a chain saw. I do what my father did, and sometimes I think he must have followed what he thought his brother and his father did. But when I read their letters from the 1930s, I think I don't know these men at all.

I don't hunt because I've never been very good at it. Waiting dutifully and motionless in now-illegal hunting stands near Brownville Junction, I sensed nothing but the growing November cold. This cannot be Maine for real. I did not inherit the patience of my father, who never hunted, but whose neuroses suddenly vanished as the sights aligned in his calmed hands.

I don't fish because each amateurish cast reminds me

how much less dedicated I am than my immigrant grandfather, who came from Sweden and fished those western
streams into the sterility you find them in today. My uncle
settles a fly twenty yards away on the concentric circles of
a rise. My line splashes erratically over the surface.

I don't hike much because hiking is a slow and tedious
thing and too many graduates of too many Outdoor Leader-
ship Schools and Outward Bound programs lecture me on
wool and proper socks and underwear and brook no devia-
tions from their fire-building and bum-wiping ideologies.
On the day I first met Linda Jane, I hiked bored and alone
to the nearest high ridge with a name on the topographical
map. I took off my boots and continued barefoot and naked,
the hammers of the menfolk now silenced by the deep
Maine woods, the ridge dry, like the hills of the San Gabriels
in California. Sailing, even in the coldest June, I strip down
in the night air and walk as deftly as I can around the deck.

I don't ski or sled or strap on snowshoes because I am
now a seasonal resident of Maine and I rarely see the snow
except on the mountains surrounding Los Angeles. When I
was last here for the winter, I taught myself to figure skate
on the contrived ice of hockey rinks in southern Maine, and
I may as well have been in Rochester, Tulsa, or Ontario.

I play Maine with boats, while others cut wood, and others grow vegetables and study the readings of thermome-
ters in compost heaps, and others kill things, and others
march deep into the winter woods. They speak the language
of these things, and form their phrases carefully, in ways

that won't embarrass them or earn a reprimand from a teacher, lover, or an editor. As I warm myself in the hunting shack in Brownville Junction, the old Maine hunter enters with his rifle held at the hips; it is aimed directly at the chest of a friend beside me, his name made famous by his family's shoe company. "That thing loaded?" he asks. And this authentic Maine man, now in his midfifties, answers: "Safety's on. Safety's on."

This is a book about sailing, and I could thus just begin with some grand metaphor about leaving a dock or harbor or an anchorage, or perhaps detail the origins of my history with sailing. I could discuss the lives of my ancestors—my grandfather, father, and my uncle Duke, who sailed with Byrd to Antarctica and talked of nothing but his glory days playing football for Exeter. But sailing, as I have experienced it, has never lent itself to such histories. And to discuss it in this fashion is to fall victim to the language of sailing magazines and the dangerous nostalgia of traditional cruising guides. Instead I think: I sail alone; I sail with others; and I sail with Linda Jane.

She is on the tiller, the curve of her cheek like the curve of the hull itself. The boat is heeled over. I think, watching Linda Jane, how the feel of the boat moving so quickly through the water on a late May afternoon was once terrifying to me. But "terror" is the wrong word for this. There is no word for this in the old sailor's perfect lexicon. She purses her lips in oblivion as the bow cuts its daysail course toward Hope Island, southwest of Chebeague.

PART I
SOUTHERN COAST

CHAPTER ONE

PORTSMOUTH

Yet another incomparably beautiful anchorage.
—Gnomic utterance recorded 1993

The first port on the southern coast of Maine is Kittery; it faces Portsmouth across the Piscataqua River, which divides Maine from New Hampshire. Years ago I lived a year of married life in New Hampshire, a river-band away from Maine. Here, I came close to forgetting Maine as I learned to cook, and kept house, and walked down to the river every evening to do some fly-fishing in unconscious imitation of that branch of my family now in Colorado. If this were a coming-of-age story or romance, my life in Portsmouth would be the end point, the bourgeois life for which all my adolescence served as prelude. But it is rather the beginning. I planned to leave Linda Jane in Portsmouth, with her horses and cuckoldings, and leave with her the coast of Maine as well. I would go south, to New Orleans, the most foreign place I would ever know. This is the kind of thing young people do. I would become, I thought, something of a novelist, although I didn't know the novels I would write, and I had no idea what lives such people as novelists led, nor what they did to gain access to such lives. I simply skimmed their paragraphs and imagined I could do better.

Preparing for this future, about which I knew nothing, I drove not south at all but east, Down East as it turned out, to collect and read my notes and type my drafts and contemplate grand schemes of things with my now-dead friend James.

James came back from Vietnam as he had left for Vietnam, directionless, obtuse, and finally grotesquely fat. He stayed in a family cottage in Cutler, which is nearly as far from the southern coast of Maine as you can get and still be on the coast of Maine. He used an outhouse, a badly tended one, and hand-pumped water from the well to the kitchen. As I typed my drafts, he lay in bed, smoking marijuana he had brought back from Vietnam (he claimed), and read and reread copies of letters he had written when he was overseas. Letter after letter. Day after day. He smoked. He imagined the actors who would play the parts of our fictions. He played chess, with unspeakable slowness, fifteen to twenty minutes for each pedestrian move. I read Camus and played bad losing moves in seconds. He died while running in a local road race for some charity organized in Machias, if Machias was ever a place for charity, back when both running road races and dying itself seemed extraordinary.

When I left Linda Jane, or planned to leave her, she took in a roommate to replace me. A heavy-limbed, small-waisted, well-hipped hippie girl, it seemed, rust hair and skin, and long fingernails she used to stroke you without so much as touching you with her fingertips. I took her room-mate, this other Linda Jane, down to the Piscataqua in the evening. It was the last week I would spend in New Hampshire. We swam in the summer water in the shadow of the newly completed bridge.

That was my bridge, I thought. My bridge. I had worked on that bridge, or around that bridge, as one of the indolent underemployed who had replaced the real workers in the last two weeks of the project. I made $200 "looking busy," as one does on such crews, and I did not work again for months. Linda Jane ran her fingernails across my chest. In those days, you just threw your clothes on the bank and walked into the water. We workers beautified the highway, we were told, by hiding unsightly loose rocks behind the bushes of the newly completed roadway. You can still find them there behind the trunks of fully grown trees lining Interstate 95 if you stop to look for them.

Whenever I have driven home, from New Orleans, from the Midwest, from California, I have crossed that bridge. The light drifts up the river from Kittery and Portsmouth. I look down and catch a glimpse of two young lovers swimming in the warm river.

The river is a place of beginning Maine and leaving Maine. The river was where I came home to Linda Jane and left her for New Orleans. It was where I saw her for nearly the last time after driving, as it turned out, the entire coast of Maine from New Hampshire to Cutler and back, unknowingly roughing out the route I would later sail so many times. For a week, James reread his words in Cutler. I was leaving my married life, watching James read those letters, but we were all kids and didn't pretend such things as marriage commitments or breaking them mattered much. But even I was finally bored with the monotone laughter over the too-often-read letters.

Returning to New Hampshire, I drove hours to the southwest; I did not know then that this is against the direction of the prevailing winds in summer. There was no phone. I imagined I could stop in Brunswick and see an older Linda Jane, and thirty-five was older then. She had read my draft of juvenile fiction and pretended to like it. I was the most easily manipulated lover she had ever had. But that evening, she had others to attend to and the phone rang and, unanswered, rang and rang.

Portsmouth was an expensive long-distance call; and you do not need to announce your return to where you pay the rent. I drove into the parking lot of the apartment complex by the Piscataqua and walked up the path to the doorway. Every time I step in dog droppings, whatever name I give them, dog turds, doo, poop, whatever, I think of that day. Paris, a schoolyard, a walkway—it is always that particular day. I walked into my apartment and may have knocked. I was greeted not by my wife but by her roommate Linda Jane—large-hipped hippie girl that she was. She had the same uneasy smile she had the night we swam in the river, the same uneasy smile she showed on a later day stroking me. She never quite caught your eye. "I stepped in something." I began washing the soles of my boots in the kitchen. Linda Jane stood quietly and in embarrassment. Two boys hardly my own age came downstairs together, walking with unusual care. They left uneasily and unsmilingly. Or perhaps I can see one of them smiling in the most perfunctory of ways. One had been with Linda Jane; the other had been in the second bedroom with my wife. I do not know how I would have acted in their situation. In Brunswick, a few weeks earlier, the violent lover of the thirty-five-year-old Linda Jane knocked on the door in the early morning. "Put on your shoes," she said. She talked him out of his suspicions as he stood in the doorway and I never saw him. I kept cleaning my boots. My wife and Linda Jane stood together in silence. Maybe they were guilty or embarrassed. That was the sort of thing that happened in New Hampshire.

THE DELIVERY

The next time I was on the river dividing Maine from New Hampshire was to pick up the boat I still own. This is a traditional twenty-seven-foot Alberg-designed sloop that looks precisely as boats are imagined to look (but did not) decades ago. It is said to sleep four, as many boats this size are said to. But four people will never sleep in that cabin unless they appreciate the torture of sailing in the eighteenth century.

To say I sail a traditional sloop means that I operate a machine of the high modern period designed in the 1940s.

It has a simple sail plan, so it is said, simple in the sense that a Corbusier building is simple, with its high modern efficiency and cleanliness of line. These waxed white, Marconi-rigged, low-maintenance sloops with small self-bailing cockpits designed for single-handed sailing were unknown in the nineteenth century, which favored, even in their working boats, then-efficient gaff-rigged wooden sloops with multiple jibs, a bowsprit, running backstays, and complex rigging. Today, such boats are known with some fear and condescension as "character boats."

My traditional boat has a traditional Danforth anchor designed not for small sailing boats but for World War II landing craft, with several hundred feet of late-twentieth-century 3/8" nylon anchor rode, undersized, some summer cruisers scoff, but so strong you could lift the boat with it. The Dacron sails have the full battens popularized in the 1980s. The jibs are "hanked on," whereas those in most comparable boats furl more conveniently on the forestay. You cannot transform this machine into a character boat, but you can operate it that way. You can sail as the schooner captain sails, anchoring under sail in the light wind with the onlookers muttering, "A bit much, that is." And you can change headsails the old way, wrestling the crackling composites to the bow as the boat luffs up into the wind.

Of course this is all *a bit much;* even the description is *a bit much.* Because as I have often said, imitating David on the fishing boat, denouncing hydraulic winches in favor of "hauling by hand with the niggerhead": "Why I guess when I'm so damn old and feeble I can't get to the bow and douse my own headsails, why then"—I say, quoting now directly—"I guess I'll just go do something else." And I have kept that vow, I will then add, speaking now in my own voice, and that something else I do, as you can guess, is called "sailing with modern furling," like all the rest.

The word "traditional" used of my boat is thus misapplied. There is nothing traditional in a larger historical sense about a fiberglass hull, an aluminum mast, stainless steel standing rigging and toggles, composite sails, and a diesel engine. Wood, that material of life, whether burned in a woodstove or shaped into sheathing, grows to maturity, then is cut and weathered and on boats will one day rot on the water. No one yet knows what the life of fiberglass will be.

So I have come to use the word "traditional" in an ironic sense. I have come to use it in answer to such questions as, "How does one anchor?" "Well, the *traditional* way involves a husband and wife. The wife is on the wheel, the husband on the bow with a large COR anchor attached to too much chain. The husband struggles with the anchor, which, as a younger man, he believes he could have handled with ease; in accordance with established *tradition*, he yells unintelligible commands to his wife and blames her for all that goes wrong."

But the word "traditional" must mean something more than this. If it has an ironic sense, it must have an ordinary sense as well. And thus the boat design from the early twentieth century, its rebirth in the hull molds of the 1970s, and

the contemporary bad captaining of an auxiliary sloop—
these things are all crude variants of an imagined primary.
When we long for the traditional, when we use the word itself, here in these Maine summers, just what is it we wish
to imagine?

My boat is a larger version of the fleet of Sea Sprites
now moored off MacMahan Island and sailed by Linda
Jane's father. All are variants of the first small boat I sailed.
That too was Alberg-designed, thus a classic or traditional
Maine sailing sloop, and you can find it lying in disuse beneath a blown-out cover in a yard not three miles from
where I sit right now. I am always unsettled to see it there,
although I cannot help but point it out to anyone walking
the point with me.

I replaced that now-idle boat because buying a larger
boat was something I thought one did, and possibly because I imagined it would get me closer to the kind of sailing Charlie and Nancy did, who had introduced me to
sailing generally and the operation of full-keeled sloops. I
could, I imagined, sail up and down the coast, firing up the
burbling diesel when the wind died. And in fact, I now do
that, but with far less diesel than I imagined then, and not
as the person I then imagined would do all this. Sailing
Down East is something for which Linda Jane must take
credit, not the boat itself, but even that is years away.

Changing boats, moving up in boats, that is, exchang-
ing my small boat for a larger one, for me—for the me that
was me then—was, quite simply, a mistake. I did what I

thought "was done," not what I wanted to do; or perhaps I had been talked into it, or perhaps I was living out some fantasy of Maine tradition that may not have even been my fantasy. And there must have been a woman involved in all of it—Linda Jane—and it hardly mattered who this woman was or what our future was together. Like leaving Maine for New Orleans. Like laughing at the boys in bed with my wife and with Linda Jane. Like listening to a doomed Vietnam veteran reading his doomed old letters. Angry with myself, having bought that boat, I drove again to Kittery, to the river separating Maine from Portsmouth, remembering that other foolish drive to Portsmouth years ago.

My new boat was on the dock. It seemed to chide me, ill-named as it was, and though it seemed well maintained, I never quite trusted the previous owner's relation to "Elmer," as he insistently called the owner of Dion's Yacht Yard, as if he enjoyed some special privileges among its workforce. So I thought that this would not be a sail at all, any more than the last drive to Portsmouth had been a return to my marriage or even a return to the rusty-tanned Linda Jane, with her fingers slowly and methodically and with obvious practice stroking my chest. This would be a mere "delivery." Two days. I would assume the role not of a sailor with a new boat but of a worker moving one. I had not then seen what a real delivery was: the single-handed workman desecrating the anchorage at Trafton Island Down East, the banality of his curses meant to persuade those anchored nearby that things usually went better.

For a delivery, one must travel light, so I thought, playing Maine, and I left my sleeping bag home and my box of food home and reading materials home and extra clothes home and it would take two days, I thought, of easy sailing Down East, as they say, meaning downwind to the east with the prevailing winds. Or maybe I just left those things in the car in Dion's parking lot for "Elmer." It would not be worth the trouble, I must have thought, to carry them down to the dock for the delivery.

The weather was wrong, and there were twenty-five-knot winds from the south, so it was pointless, I let myself think, to try to work my way up the coast in the late afternoon, to motor into an unfamiliar harbor in the twilight on that flat coast, its beach after beach with the narrow, barely navigable rivers separating them: York and Cape Porpoise and Kennebunk—all crowded with boats and navigational buoys before you reach what amounts to the rocky coast of Maine north and east of Portland.

It is late afternoon and it is late August and, I realize absurdly, it is also the anniversary of my long-past marriage. I found Linda Jane in the arms of her best girlfriend on the eve of my wedding and thought nothing of it then and think nothing of it now. What I remember is walking with the two of them a week earlier in the twilight, with my arms around each of them and stroking her best friend in the August darkness of northern Maine. It was so far from the coast, in that northern wooded section of Maine, and most of the people I knew there hunted, or took drugs, or eventually brought their guns and drugs to the coast and took up commercial fishing. They took up commercial fishing before they went broke like most people in that business and limped back to inland Maine to work in the woods. And amidst them, my Linda Jane lay with her friend with her hippie glasses (whose hippie glasses?) carefully placed on the night table.

I watched them there; a week earlier, I had driven from her North Woods to my coast, again delivering—furniture, was it? or maybe tack for the horses. Even now, I recall thinking that I should continue driving, down the coast, past New Hampshire and its cuckoldings and into the bowl of the Midwest and finally south or maybe northwest to Alaska and never head back to the Maine woods and Linda Jane, my wife-to-be.

It would be another year, just past our anniversary, before I actually made that drive south to Louisiana. I had by then lived my year of married life with its attendant securities; I had worked on a construction crew, I had written my novels, and I had spent most of the money I made on the fishing boats. I ended my drive finally in New Orleans, and I would look for work I never found or very much wanted on the shrimp boats in Houma. I am dozing off in my car, near the Morning Call coffee shop on Decatur Street; I am lost and in tears. This too was a mistake, I think. This southing, as the old navigators called it; these cities. I wake to a small fist rapping on the glass; it is the frail hitchhiker I had picked up in Mississippi days earlier. He took me to

Buster's on Burgundy Street, I think, where you could eat for thirty-five cents and life was grand again. But that was years earlier, as the south wind blew, and now there was nothing but the new boat and the last weeks of sailing season and the seventy-mile delivery north from Portsmouth.

I spent the first night on the boat on the wharf and the next morning I motored out of Portsmouth Harbor. There is a buoy marking the first point off Dion's wharf; that buoy marks a rock that lies somewhat shallower than keelboats can negotiate at low tide; it would be two weeks before I realized I had taken that buoy on the wrong side; it was only the rising tide that kept me from spending the second night as well at the wharf at Dion's Yacht Yard. The next spring, on my first sail of that year, I would have the slim and calloused Linda Jane aboard. As I explained to her the location of another ledge, much like the hidden ledge off Dion's wharf, we hit that very ledge at hull speed on a falling tide. We would spend eight hours there, most of it high and dry; we would get the boat off two hours before midnight. The photo of the boat set jauntily on the ledge still embarrasses me, but Bill Sr. at the marina put it best: "Could have been next weekend for all the tourists on Memorial Day." The next day, the boat is on the mooring; I laugh with Linda Jane in the cabin in the chop and swells and we pretend that this incident hardly matters. Or perhaps it was not the next day, or perhaps it was not Linda Jane at all.

As I sailed up from Portsmouth, I passed the spots I knew from my childhood, looking out into the great sweep of ocean. Cape Neddick and, distantly, Boon Island, where Kenneth Roberts describes the cannibalism of the wrecked crew I read about summer after summer after summer. In early afternoon, I put in, as they say, to the Kennebunk River, another place of my childhood. I thought, motoring up the river, I could recognize Great Hill, with my uncle's cottage, and I knew farther up the river was the hand-operated drawbridge (or once was), and I could still smell the fish market next to it, where my mother would buy us exotic fare like swordfish or crabmeat or mackerel. "Tinker mackerel," she always insisted these mere mackerel were.

I brought the boat to the dock and stepped off. But I had never operated a boat of any kind in a river, and I now know you need to have a line ready and you need to make that line fast to the dock before the boat loses what is called its way. Otherwise, the river will simply take your boat away downriver as it almost took mine. Maybe that's why I nearly snapped once at Linda Jane as she stood on a neighbor's dock, firmly holding both ends of the consequently useless dockline.

Holding the rail as the river ran insistently east, I wondered whether I should just let the boat go, as I had finally let my life with Linda Jane go, and stand helplessly on the wharf, and begin my new life, boatless and landlocked, or whether I should hold on as it dragged me from the wharf and try heroically to board. I thought all that as the weak river currents pulled the boat rail away from me, stalled, and the hull settled back into the wharf. No one was watching, or I saw no one watching. So no one would witness or understand that my new life began on that day and perhaps at that moment. I was early, and lucky to get one of the three moorings in the river. The next two dozen boats would raft up on the wharf in the rain.

It blew from the east and then hard from the north and east. By late afternoon on this Labor Day weekend, the boats were rafted up six deep on the wharf and they did not move for days. I slept in my sailbag and carefully rationed the single loaf of bread I brought. I recovered from my snuff addiction, and tied intricate knots with the spare line. I thought of Linda Jane at work in Harpswell; Linda Jane whom I barely knew, but who would doubtless go sailing with me if only I could get this boat to Casco Bay. I think now of her hard, working hands and the way she would trace misspelled messages on my back. The next morning it blew from the northeast again. I motored to the mouth of the river and could not motor through the chop as the river met the wind. Three days I sat on the mooring in the wind, cold, wrapped in the sailbag and finally the sail itself, listening on the marine-band radio to those anchored at Jewell Island who did not understand why they were dragging anchor in what all the guidebooks assured them was a secure anchorage despite the soft mud bottom. To them, the promise of security was more authoritative than wind direction, as the wind funneled through the north-facing opening with gusts, they claimed, to fifty knots. Maybe they will read of their predicament today.

I slept in my sailbag as those in the well-equipped cruising boats anchored at Jewell Island and rafted up six deep at the wharf at Chicks Marina did not. I knew I had made a mistake, not just in buying the boat in the first place, but in envisioning my trip home with it. I knew now that no true boat-deliverer would ever plan on his own discomfort and indifference as I had done. I realized that this was no delivery, but merely playing at delivery, playing badly, it turned out; and it was not being in Maine but simply a halting and failed step in playing Maine. No man works for a living who has a means of living. And the wind howled relentlessly through the rigging.

I watched the rust work down from the chainplates. I would rebed that chainplate the next year with a torque wrench with Linda Jane bent over me, her hard chest rubbing against my shoulder. Years later I realized that the unbedded chainplate was a sign of a pernicious history, of real damage to the hull, which the owner had not bothered to reveal. I would realize that all blemishes have histories, even the most inconsequential of them. An accident, a moment of neglect that is itself a sign of other moments of neglect.

Yet in time, despite the chicaneries or simple negligence of the owner, that boat became worth more than anything I could have paid for it, as the cold and irritation and embarrassment of those days grew distant and as Linda Jane's strong hands grasped the winch handle and she leaned over the rail intent on the genoa. We sailed one evening around

Haskell Island the following season and those same hands held my belt and the boat seemed to sail itself through the tide and past the buoys.

There is a monkey's fist I tied now stowed uselessly on one of the few shelves of the boat, and it remains there to remind me of all my mistakes, which seem epitomized by this one. As Linda Jane leans over me the following spring, as we lie on the starboard berth, as she leans over me years later in the darkness, anchored in some cove west of Vinalhaven, I see the monkey's fist on the shelf and she says and she says, deafly, she says . . .

Once out of the Piscataqua River in Portsmouth, you turn north up the coast of Maine, and until you reach Casco Bay what you have is a long stretch of sandy beaches. There are islands—Boon Island, far offshore, where the wrecked crew ate seaweed and gulls and finally each other. And there are lighthouses, like Cape Neddick, and places like Ogunquit. To me, Ogunquit is not a place at all, but an incident: I am being awakened from a drunken sleep at age seventeen; I am pulled from the backseat of my car parked somehow in a neighbor's driveway, and I then tell I think my irate father I am on my way to Ogunquit to deliver chickens. My mother cried to see me, I am told, drunk and on my way to Ogunquit. But I never in my life saw such things from her.

I was on my way to Ogunquit because I did in fact deliver chickens in those days, door-to-door in southern

Maine, to the now-famous Bush compound on Walker's Point and places on Prouts Neck where I went in the servants' entrance and was fed by black cooks. I was a bad salesman and the only redeeming aspect of my work was driving the old Saab with the bald tires at ninety miles an hour, and thinking how Mrs. Berry of Merrymeeting Farm, with all the sanguinity of Chaucer's Cook, guiltlessly carved the green rot from the top of the frozen livers and cheerily refroze them for her customers without so much as reweighing the package. Such were the delicacies known to the rich summerfolk of Prouts Neck and Ogunquit. And there was nothing of note in all this but the absurdity of doing it in the first place and all that travel—to Falmouth and Cape Porpoise and Biddeford Pool and all those posh harbors I now can sail to, but never do.

When the weather cleared after my three nights in the sailbag, I left Kennebunk and sailed to Richmond Island, which looks on the chart like a secure and easy anchorage but which I am fortunate not to have reached three days earlier. From there, the islands of the Maine coast finally appear. The wind died and I motored with the single-cylinder diesel burbling not quite as silently as I had imagined through the calm to the middle of those islands in Harpswell, thinking only of that storm and the smell of Kennebunk some thirty years earlier and the strong hands of Linda Jane that I might now look forward to.

It was early September and there would be less than three weeks left in the season, as Hurricane Gloria formed deep in the Atlantic. Its destruction, which should have brought some prelapsarian peace to this area, brought instead three days of roaring generators and chain saws, and it would be too late for me and Linda Jane. She would be lost in her work, in her young child, in her family, and I would be running away from Maine to Los Angeles again.

The boat is ashore. It is secure on the chained stands of the boatyard. The hurricane has disappeared into the westerlies over Nova Scotia, and I am leaving for Los Angeles. And it is that day, I believe, on my way to Los Angeles, that I would begin these two parallel histories—the history of the boat, and the history of Linda Jane, then lost out there somewhere in Nebraska. I drove west, this time, relentlessly west, thinking of the strong hands of Linda Jane. Thinking of my weeklong drive to the West Coast. Only this would not be a weeklong drive to the West Coast, but two weeks, three weeks, or what seemed like more.

And still, she awaits me there, on the phone to her adoring husband, exiled there in Nebraska, as I drive, unknowingly, to her door.

CHAPTER TWO

KENNEBUNK BEACH

It was [then] . . .
That the grapes seemed fatter.
The fox ran out of his hole.

—Wallace Stevens

Kennebunk is typical of the geography of the southern coast, its long beaches broken periodically by such features as Walker's Point, where, at the Bush compound, I delivered chickens to the help. There are houses like that up and down the coast; we feel nostalgia for the older ones and criticize the newer ones that do not conform to them. There is a marginally navigable river running past Chicks Marina and ending at the drawbridge in Kennebunkport. It is where my traditional boat almost drifted free in the currents to leave me helpless and alone on a late August day. Somewhat less navigable is the Mousam River in Kennebunk Beach, with my uncle's cottage backed onto its eastern branch. All those cottages used to dump raw sewage into those picturesque rivers, a practice still, I find, a touchy subject among longtime residents.

Kennebunk, as I learned from the scrawls of handwritten maps drawn by my former employer, the Chicken Lady, is three towns. Her customers, who, incredibly, bought the chickens delivered door-to-door to them, are divided among those three towns into three groups. The Port, with its large, ocean-facing estates and occasional good appetite for chicken. Then the wealthier, more self-assured Kennebunk itself, with large Victorian houses, one once owned by my dead, suicidal uncle (not really an uncle, but a gay old blade from the old days, I suppose). Then finally the Beach, with its long stretches of sand and cobblestone, beaches not quite so expansive as they seemed to me more than fifty years ago. The cottages, some of them old, are more modest here, and here no one bought much of anything from the Chicken Lady.

Facing one of those cobblestone beaches is a small and once-typical Victorian cottage, its gingerbread trim, carefully depicted in two paintings from the late nineteenth century, now stripped away. This cottage was built by one of my namesakes and passed on, somewhat circuitously, I'm told, to my father's cousin. This was the man I was named after, a white-haired irascible man who died friendless of emphysema. I loved him because I loved the smell of the old wood-paneled Victorian cottage with the sweeping porches and I loved the way he never blamed us children for the rules we broke and the equipment and tools we inevitably misused. Although for me, the gulf between the adult world and our own could not be bridged by names alone, for him, that name sharing was enough. For the name alone, then, he was grateful and thus listened, sitting on the porch, to my father's stories, embellished, doubtless, since Father in those days did not yet husband the gin as surreptitiously as he later would.

As Uncle Joe attended to Father's meandering and duplicitous stories, he knew, I imagine, all about the gay old days of the 1930s on the Beach with the swells. Father, and the cousins, and the Lords, and the men all dressed up in the photographs with their 1930s swimsuits. All those gay old days of the 1930s. I doubt Joe much participated in them, although perhaps it is just his name that makes me think that. I see them in the old photos, arms folded across their narrow chests and dark swimsuits, the contrived insouciance of their smiles. No one explained to me those photographs, pasted in the books next to the others: your aunt Marcia, your uncle Duke, your grandfather, the house on Highland Avenue, Uncle Frank at your christening. Just a line of young men with their careless smiles and their poses too somehow physical for the backdrop of my awful grandmother's photo album.

There are no stories to tell of Uncle Joe, since he revealed so little of his life. Each week he visited the grave of his wife; we watched him stare and tried to be part of it. We children knew he owned the cottage, and we knew he bought a new car every other year back when that was considered an American thing to do. We did not know what adults knew of him, nor what adults thought of him, nor why we were able to use this cottage for weeks in the summer, nor whether there was any financial arrangement, nor what all this name sharing meant.

The cars he drove were big and heavy, as the grandest cars were of the 1950s; the upholstery of these cars was slick and smelled like our own cars never smelled nor how I ever remembered them to smell. The slick upholstery was red, and at least one of these cars had a convertible top. The bumpers were enormous chrome slabs, and when we returned to the cottage the next summer, these reds and slabs of chrome might well be replaced by others. He was an architect. I know this because I was told this. His voice showed the early signs of emphysema. I know this because I was told this. When he died, he left me a small sum twice what he left my brother and my sister. I remember the sum, but I cannot remember the circumstances of his death, just a trip to the cottage during the school year, and Joe somewhat more taciturn than usual. Was I twelve? Had we outgrown the cottage of my childhood summers? Who else was so unusually reserved that day? Who would grieve for him? The dyings of those who share your name were things my family spared me, the dyings of those who loved you. I have returned to that cottage in recent years, decades after his death, and little about it has changed. The waist-high console radio is gone.

He had a heavy wooden boat with a Johnson 5hp that at the right tide coinciding with his weekend visit coinciding with favorable weather would mean a trip up the Mousam

River, filled with its sewage from rich summer residents. I was never good with the motorboat and when given the controls on the handle of the outboard, I turned hard port and drove my father's face into the water. He came up sputtering and for some reason, all I can remember is my fear that he might have lost his glasses. But why were glasses of such importance in the 1950s?

THE DOGFISH

When we found the dogfish, the mysterious kids who showed it to us stood astride it as if flexing their muscles growing suddenly in puberty. Dogfish are sharks two to three feet long and have two large spines on their dorsal fins. We were assured that these spines are poisonous. The kids were the kind I generally avoided, since they would bully me or otherwise ridicule whatever solitude I found there. These kids did none of that, didn't shove my face into the rotting flesh, nor drive my hands onto the poisonous spines, sparing me all that, I imagined at some point, due to my own childish admiration of them. I brought my father and let us say I also brought my uncle down to the rocks where we found the dogfish; and I say my uncle joined us because I wanted him to join us in things like that, or now wish him to join, because in life, in the real and mysterious life he led, he never did such things.

There was a story told, perhaps by my father, perhaps by another adult if there was one, always a story, about a man in the water and some military boat, always the military motif in every story men told in the 1950s. A story told while the kids stood astride the mutilated fish. And now that I recall it, there are other details in the story explaining how this mythical soldier got in the water—an unmanned boat being towed and the line parting and the man diving in to retrieve the drifting boat. I can see the man in the water, and seeing it, can reimagine the narrative that places him there. There is a key detail of the story that the adult teller most reveled in (was this man my father? how long has it been too late to ask?): the soldier suddenly cries out, "Shoot me. Shoot me. I'm being eaten by dogfish." And there, the story ends. My uncle held the silence he had held throughout the telling of the story, not because the story was implausible, but because its ending could not be told at all: American men, particularly military men, did not shoot other American men. And at that time, there were no American men but military men. And that was the story. We had seen the proof of this story in the dead fish on the rock beach.

All the details I know are impossible. They are impossible as I have remembered them, impossible as they must have been told: men do not dive from military boats to retrieve parted lines, and men are not routinely armed in boats near dogfish, and men in the water are not easily heard above the engine noise, nor do they articulate their thoughts as did the soldier in the water. I could add, I suppose, as further implausible details, those unseen kids who appeared on the beach that day, and the curious uncle who never followed us out on the beach. Yet against all that was the mutilated fish—proof of any story that would be told that day. We walked back across the pebbled beach and I thought about the knife cuts at the dorsal fins where the kids I never saw again had cut out the poisonous spines.

When I first worked on the lobster boat in the summer of 1967, it was a great year for dogfish. You would catch them with your lures just beneath the surface, always fishing for something else, and they would take your line slowly so slowly and deliberately out. Some of the old story of the doomed soldier must have stayed with me, because we always left these slow and deliberate fish dead for the gulls, as if it were the moral or civic thing to do. As if another brave soldier swimming to retrieve a parted line might one day be spared the unspeakable death of that soldier in the water.

Why, David asked, would you work on the boat all day, ass-deep in the bait box, then spend the evening back on the water fishing like summerfolk? Why too, I might have answered, would working fishermen like him stow their gear on Saturday and spend their Sundays chasing bluefin tuna?

A dogfish is harmless to swimmers, but will bull its way into a lobster trap and as large as it is, must coil up just to fit in the bait compartment. There it causes much damage, slashing, I suppose, if the slow and deliberate fish can be said to slash, at the twine-tied heads and cutting in them huge holes that take time (that irretrievable time on a working boat) to repair. This vandal savagery is likely a matter of the dogfish relentlessly pushing and pushing on, since sharks, unique I think among the fishes, must keep moving to circulate water through their gills. David, the fisherman I worked for, killed them by cutting off their tails. In later years, reconsidering, he merely slashed, as humans slash, their bellies; this might improve the fish's futile mobility, he reasoned, and perhaps as other fish (the dreaded dogfish of the military tale) attacked it, it would wound one, and the newly wounded fish would wound another, and the cycle would rid the seas of trap-slashing dogfish. It reminded me of the image of a roomful of mousetraps, each set with a Ping-Pong ball. A ball is thrown into the room. Within seconds, each trap would spring. This was meant to illustrate nuclear chain reactions. We children were supposed, I think, to find something reassuring about that, something that adults could explain for us, but I never connected it with the nuclear blasts it was meant to depict until much later.

There was of course no killing off these innocent fish then, not by the methods we used on the lobster boat, any more than smashing the crabs that got into traps set in the wrong place would keep the traps from filling with them when you set them in the wrong place again. There was no killing dogfish off even with the inaccurate legends of their viciousness. What killed them off was a different and more sordid myth.

When the East Coast fisheries collapsed due to the predictable stupidities of overfishing consequent on greed or government interference or the plodding of the biologists, there was an attempt to save these industries by the same means that had destroyed them, that is, by overfishing. So the fisheries invented a new name for the dogfish—cape shark—and sold the delicious steaks under that name, that is, when they were not selling it under the name "sword-fish," since the two are just close enough to fool you on the ice beds of the fish market. Yet dogfish have a life cycle that is too complex for the banalities of overfishing and name changing. The females bear live young (as lobstermen who slash them know) after a two-year gestation period, and it takes those young a decade to mature. Within a year or two of overfishing, the dogfish was nearly extinct, and I haven't seen one in the water in over thirty years.

1954

I cried all morning that day in 1954. The radio is on, the now-antique console radio with the semicircular dial, and we are being told of an approaching storm, a "hurricane." It is a word I had never heard.

I had seen the tornado in *The Wizard of Oz;* driving through Kansas decades later, desperate to see Linda Jane, I am still terrified by this image. A hurricane was not like that, I was assured. Not like that at all. Yet we packed and drove to Kennebunk, to the large Victorian house of my kind but finally suicidal uncle Frank. There, in the well-built turreted Victorian, we would be safe. I don't remember the wind at all. I remember that when the wind died we walked outside among the fallen tree trunks crisscrossed on the lawn. My father and brother drove back to the Beach to find the cobblestones blown up over the road and blocking it. When they returned, the great elms on Summer Street began to fall.

That is the story.

They had been, they would later say, in the eye of the hurricane. They had not known that when the east wind stopped in the clearing sky, it would return from the west with equal force. How could they know? Or so they said at the time. Yet I ask myself again, how could they know? How could this story, so well remembered, be true? What was it that my older brother, sitting in the bed next to mine as I woke up, what was the story he told me? of the cobblestones heaped up on the road to Great Hill, and the surf as high as the telephone wires?

I have been through a number of storms since then, and I have checked the path of Hurricane Carol on the public records from NOAA. I know now that this familial tale cannot be accurate—the trees falling on Summer Street while the surprised family drove back from Kennebunk Beach as the eye passed. I have no recollection of their leaving that day, just the walking in the afternoon on the downed trees, or perhaps I remember only telling of walking on the downed trees. A hurricane passes at about thirty miles per hour on the Maine coast. The eye can be no more than a few miles wide. There is hardly time while the eye passes at such a speed even to plan what one will do, let alone drive to the Beach and back.

Hurricanes of course defy the conventions of tales and memory. If a hurricane passes exactly to the east, its forward movement to the north and east can perfectly match the counterclockwise rotational wind speed on the west, and you will seem becalmed. During a hurricane in the fall of 2008, I nervously watched my boat on its untrusted mooring in front of my house. The hurricane passed to the east, with its core winds at forty-five to sixty knots. The northeastward track of the hurricane exactly compensated for the south-flowing air on the western quadrant. The highest breeze recorded in my anchorage was three knots.

Such oddities will happen; yet when I research the course of Hurricane Carol in 1954, the track of the storm will not support this or any other theory compatible with the details of the stories I have heard and participated in, even though many of the motifs, particularly the moralistic ones, seem perfectly in place: the eye of the storm and the opposing wind directions, the vagueness of weather reports in the 1950s, the trees down on Summer Street, the surprise of it all, the way the most experienced of sailors managed heroically to cope with it and describe it all so movingly in the sailing magazines—all those old salts caught in the hurricane due to the inadequacy of weather reporting. I read about this storm in the sailing guides, and marvel at how long ago the authors think that was.

THE COTTAGE

There is a painting on my wall of a lone Victorian cottage in Kennebunk Beach dated 1874. In the background is a deserted and barren Lord's Point, a point now covered with code-built structures that can no longer be described as cottages at all. The oldest, I believe, was built by my awful grandparents. What is for me the most familiar feature of that cottage, the long sweeping porch, was then unbuilt. The decorative trim shown in the painting is now gone, as are the useless lightning rods at each end of the roof. There are Victorian women in Victorian dresses on the beach and they can be imagined to speak as people do in Sarah Orne Jewett's *The Country of the Pointed Firs*. But the figures are not Jewett's real Victorians; they are the artificial Victorians one sees in all genre paintings of the period. On tour, vacationing, looking at monuments. There is a companion to this painting, painted by the same artist in the same year. It now hangs in the dining room of the meticulously maintained cottage it depicts. In this one, there are no Victorian figures on the beach; all the human forms are gone.

By the time I knew that cottage, it had been moved to the road to Great Hill, and now faced east over a cobblestone beach. The sand beaches in the paintings are a five-minute drive away in the old Plymouth. From the undepicted porch, you can see Mount Agamenticus to the south, just as it is drawn in the somewhat different view portrayed in the painting, or you can look east to where the

sun rises over the water and over Kenneth Roberts's canni-
bals of Boon Island.

The cottage smelled of wood paneling and mold and
beach roses and salt water. There were tiny rooms upstairs
that to a young child seemed enormous, and even the
straight corridor in the darkness strange and twisted. My
aunt or her detested parents slept at one end of the corridor,
my own parents on the other. In the middle were the door-
ways to the room where my sister slept and the wood-
paneled room with the sweet ocean smell where I slept next
to my brother. The twin beds had smooth wooden posts and
I can still feel that smoothness in my palm. There was a single window facing Great Hill; the cobblestones rolled tire-
lessly in the surf. I would wake up in the beds with no
recollection of the evening drive to Kennebunk. I have an
impossible memory associating that room with Jim Lon-
borg of the Red Sox unable to win the third game he pitched
in the 1967 World Series. It is impossible because the World
Series is in October, and we were never in Kennebunk that
late. More important, in 1967 I was twenty, and Uncle Joe is
dead I think and we have not been to the cottage in years. I
wander lost through that simple upstairs corridor suddenly
complex in a dream of it, and perhaps dreaming, in 1967, in
October 1967, recalls the summers with my brother, listening relentlessly to the Red Sox on the oversized radio or on
his then-marvelous transistor radio as he compiled a season's worth of batting statistics in a system he had invented.

From the cobblestone beach, the distinctive line of Great Hill has receded, due to erosion, not *an* erosion as, corrected by my brother, I now know. I do not recognize the sprawling estate on that hill. But my uncle's Victorian seems unchanged since I last slept there, as our own faces seem unchanged in the mirror, no matter how many decades we have stared at them. The old console radio, announcing Hurricane Carol, is off for repairs, I am told. The cement driveway, barely wide enough for one of Joe's cars, still has the white line painted down the middle; this apparent absurdity is not, I'm now told, a lane divider, but designed to guide large automobiles backing out of the driveway.

In summer, the water was fiercely cold, and we swam twice a day, no matter what the temperature, off the sand beach depicted in the paintings. It is hard for me to believe today that Father waded out past his waist into the surf each day and taught us to ride these small waves into the beach. But he must have done it, because when I came to California, I would bodysurf the larger waves into the shore as if the intervening three decades had obliterated not the skills but only the verbs used to describe such doings. As if Father still stood there in his antiquated shorts and expertly timed his dive into the shoulder-high surf.

At low tide, we would feel for the sand dollars in the sand. A child's myopia made that beach seem deserted, although such solitude is unlikely, even in the 1950s. Today, the parking is by permit only, and only on the coldest summer day is the beach as it seemed to me then. There was an ice cream stand behind the beach, and if you walked to Lord's Point you would smell the fried food I always associate with one of my loonier uncles (or so-called uncles), who lived on that point. He was one of the swimsuited insouciants of the 1930s, and turned into a huckster of all sorts of failed enterprises.

I have often wondered what Father thought, waist-high in the cold water, as he watched us there on that beach. Thinking of his old sailing days, hauled aloft to varnish the mast of the schooner in the tiny photograph. Thinking of the then-young uncles, arms crossed in their now-ridiculous swimsuits. The hushed-up suicide of Frank still years in the future. Joe half-dead from emphysema, and us soon all grown out of it.

CHAPTER THREE

PORTLAND

They're all the same.

—Linda Jane, on men

Portland is the only city in Maine I know with major streets and walkways paved in cobblestones, which, picturesque though they may be, are an impediment to everything one does. You cannot drive on them and feel you have even minimal control over your car; you cannot walk on them in comfort, particularly in flat-soled boating shoes. A woman with heels, or anything other than the crassest of walking shoes, will have even more difficulty. Barefoot kids of forty years ago must have found it intolerable. Cobblestones are for beaches. They border the sand behind my uncle's cottage in Kennebunk, I know, and the sea moss dries out on them as the sand fleas scatter beneath your feet.

There is no utility in the cobblestones. They make the entire city seem quaint. On Route 295 now, between Brunswick and Portland, the commuters pass ridiculously in the morning: living in Brunswick and working in the city, living in the city and working in Brunswick. This is no city, and Brunswick, where I grew up, is no city either, with its so-called Maine Street the "second widest in the state," or country, as I once was told so solemnly. These drivers are merely playing at commuting, playing at being those hard-bitten locals who will be watched and evaluated for authenticity by summer tourists.

When walking here, I am one of them: one of the tourists, that is. I am here, say, to eat dinner. I will pay, as others will pay, as one pays in New York or Los Angeles. The ethnicity proclaimed in the restaurant sign is not right for Maine. And I will walk on the cobblestones wondering whether I will turn an ankle, wondering not what beach these stones came from, but rather how all the rounded stones are milled, or run through the same conveyer selected for size, then set in unintelligible patterns, the individual stones interchangeable.

Linda Jane and I walk over these cobblestones of Portland. We have driven to Portland because it is not worthwhile to sail here despite what the guidebooks imply, and despite how close it is to my home mooring. You can drive and park on the street. You can wait until six and park for free, or at least you used to be able to do that. You can walk along the cobblestones as Linda Jane and I walked.

She tried to explain her hearing aid to me. I imagined it would be something magical, something I could tune to boost the dips I saw in the audiologist's charts. My hearing too would be reborn in perfection. I would taste the dragon's blood and understand the songs of birds. It would be like the perfect guide to sailing, explaining everything one would need to know. Instead, that hearing aid produced not real sound but a version of sound, like an overpriced old stereo with its sometimes beautiful allusions to the music. It was a talisman only, as I walked there with Linda Jane, promising some mythic and perfect speech.

When I took the pitifully small hearing aid from her she was instantly and completely deaf. I put it in my ear and it was not like dragon's blood at all. She looked at me and I could tell now from her eyes that there was nothing I had ever said to her that she could fully understand; that she read my lips instead, and the little nods I thought were signs of uneasiness were simply the acknowledgment of something she had caught—a word, a phrase, a sentiment. She took my arm and pressed her small breast into me. She knew we would never be together. She knew we would never fly to Venice, to Milan, to Naples—wherever it was that was depicted in those postcards she once sent to me, signed in her large capitals. She walked along the cobblestones down to the wharf and she turned against me, pressing herself against me. I whispered to her and she heard nothing, saw nothing, understood nothing.

We sail past the buoy by Haskell Island. We are a mile from the mooring. We are perhaps two miles from the mooring. In the late afternoon, we can be on that mooring in an hour. It will take twenty minutes after that to get the boat in something like order. I am next to her. She buries her face against my thighs. An hour. We are an hour from the mooring as we round the buoy. She stares at me, and

again I realize it is like walking the cobblestones of Portland. Hearing nothing, she studies my unmoving lips. I am
deeply involved in the sensations. Of the curiosity of keeping the boat in the channel. Of the curiosity of holding her
with the boat in a fair breeze. Of the time. Of the hour from
the mooring. Of the white dress. Of her ridiculously frilled
socks. Of her searching my face for a word, for a phrase,
for a sentiment. As we sailed and the buoy swept past behind us.

Then Linda Jane is in Wiscasset, suddenly reborn. Suddenly large and promiscuous as everyone seemed promiscuous in those days, as if without consequence. When we,
too, walked the cobblestones of Portland, after reading Ezra
Pound in the evergreen shade, she would never have believed she would be replaced by this slim and barely literate
working girl. Nor would she believe that soon I would
rather read books than explain them to her, that for me it
was enough to brood naively about their mysteries. I assume I said something at the airport about not being good
at goodbyes or at waiting for airline departures, or perhaps
that was a later banality. I believe she went to Alaska. Or
perhaps she had come from Alaska. She put on the loose
nightgown and stood before the fire she had built in Wiscasset. Her large form caught in the firelight. She lies in the
woods by the cabin I once built and I read *The Cantos* to
her in the shade of the pointed firs.

And now Linda Jane shivers in the cold dew of Matinicus. We have come to this most remote of great Maine

islands to watch the sun rise from the sweep of ocean to the east. Instead, impossibly it seems but of course predictably, the sun is blocked today by Wooden Ball Island. I do not want her there, and I swim in the icy water so that I will not forget this day. She is not as she was when we were last in New Orleans, when her body was so perfect and the smell of the Jax Brewery was pervasive. We sit on the levee in the warm evening breeze and stare across the river to Algiers. I reach for her cool and perfect flesh. An old violinist from the Philharmonic also stares over the water, and we wonder who or what he sees on its surfaces. Or Linda Jane now walks, perhaps through my own woods, or is it in a city somewhere, in New York, or is she sitting straddled on the bow of Charlie's Hampton? sullen and unloved like the rest?

Why is Portland where these desultory affairs play out for me? Here is where my father came, in his last cancer-stricken days. Here is where Gabor, back from San Francisco, rented his last Portland apartment. And here Linda Jane walks over the cobblestones, or she drives to the suddenly fashionable Promenade in the evening, and we watch the sailors drift through the dark. I recall being driven to this sprawling city by my father; it must be my first or second year in high school and I am too young to squander the money I wished to spend on that Gibson, I believe it was. I marveled at Marginal Way—what it must be to be an adult and to drive that road alone and without fear.

Linda Jane sits in her car in the fashionable Promenade. It is safer now in Munjoy Hill than it was in the past I imagine from my high school years. I hold her as she gazes over the water with the lights reflecting off its dark surface. The navigation lights of a sailboat glow in perfect legality; the boat is barely drifting, it seems, northward along the shore below the Promenade. Working to a mooring doubtless. Linda Jane will always be angry with me, and she feels, as we drive and sail through these traditional and familiar Maine settings, that she is a mere ornament, something else "from Maine," some other detail of "playing Maine." She cannot forgive me for this, although she struggles for years to accept it. I think then about walking on the cobblestones years earlier, when I watched her face nod arrhythmically as I formed the words and she transformed them in her mind. Did Linda Jane hear those words as she heard the words as a child, before the deafness overwhelmed her? Or did no one use those words with her as a child? And is it Linda Jane who once said to me, "Such words. You say such things"?

I am with John in the house he built in the woods of Bowdoinham. I am to meet Gabor at his apartment in Portland. Gabor has lymphoma. It will be years before I am told he had AIDS. He will die that fall, in the company, I will learn, of Linda Jane. When I teach her the rudiments of sailing, I know nothing of their friendship, and she will finally dismiss me with an elaborate rationale clearly rehearsed from a therapy session. John will also die before I write this. But on that day, John pursues me in his pickup truck and stops me a few miles from his house in Bowdoinham.

Gabor will not be in Portland, he stammers. He is visiting a friend in Brunswick. Well, not quite that. He has tried to kill himself, it is said, by idling his car in a drafty garage.

I wonder what stories I might have had, waiting for him in Portland, had he succeeded. Instead, I laugh at Gabor as he dozes in the living room. I tell him of EPA rules and catalytic converters, about which he knows nothing. You need to do better to kill yourself in the clean exhaust of these too-regulated days, I say. He laughs. It worked so well in the movies and in the news reports. A month later he will truly die, or so years later Linda Jane will tell me, suffering as he was that day afraid to suffer. I drive the cobblestone streets of Portland. I feel the car shudder, out of its element. On the boat, Gabor said to me: "I understand only that here an absolute monarchy prevails." He was content to be useless on the water, having grown up landlocked in Hungary, so he said. I drive past the long brick building on the wharf, turned into apartments for the dying young.

I would like to start here, although it is hardly a port of call for me. I can find no narrative to Portland, just incidents and the intersection of old roads. A doctor's appointment. A place I was born. School functions. Dead parents. Sports events. Interviews. A call from the draft board. Classmates at school. Music stores and expensive restaurants. I drove here with Michael and we watched the ferry from Nova Scotia land at the dock without incident. Landlocked. Walking the streets of Portland. And Linda Jane pressing against me. There is no pattern to the cobblestones.

And I write: Portland is the point where the coast breaks up into what I call the real coast of Maine—rocky, irregular, and picturesque. To the south are long impenetrable beaches, and the luxuries of the classic summerfolk. And I write: Linda Jane walks with me on the cobblestones; we imagine Maine as harboring, in these eateries, some notable urbanity. So we walk on those cobblestones, looking for a Maine that isn't there, that existed for me only, say, in New Orleans, or in my memories of working on the fishing boat, still miles to the east.

PART II

HARPSWELL

CHAPTER FOUR

BASIN COVE

The pears are not viols,
Nudes or bottles.
They resemble nothing else.

—Wallace Stevens

Heading east along the coast, the first pair of substantial peninsulas you encounter form what the United States Postal Service now defines as Harpswell. Older maps and charts record a number of communities scattered over these two peninsulas: Harpswell Center, the inevitable North, South, East, and West Harpswells, Cundys Harbor, Gurnet, Orr's Island and Bailey Island, and that is still how most residents define where they live. Until the 1980s and the construction of the Ewin Narrows Bridge, the only way to get from one peninsula to the other was to drive all the way to Brunswick, a town so distant that if you were raised there, even forty years of residence will not make you a local in Harpswell. For those who lived, say, in South Harpswell, near my house, or anywhere in Bailey Island, to get to the other side of town required a twenty-minute drive just to get faced in the right direction. Long before the Ewin

Narrows Bridge, I worked on the east side of Harpswell, and because of that, I sometimes see these peninsulas (wrongly, of course) as representing the two cultures defined in the old paintings and in various guidebooks as that of hardworking locals and idling summerfolk. My drive from what is now my summer home to the wharf at Cundys Harbor to begin work took me forty-five minutes, and I would usually arrive there an hour before dawn.

FATHER AND OLDFATHER

In 1937 my father graduated from Bowdoin and went overseas to dig for archaeological gold near the Parthenon. He would attend the University of Illinois in the fall, and by a circuitous route, the letters of his future graduate school advisor, impossibly named "Oldfather," have come to me. To pitch this story, my colleague Leo warns, the name must of course be changed. These letters were among papers carefully preserved by a librarian I met in a summer seminar at the Rare Book School in Virginia. Linda Jane was in that class as well, and years later, herself impossibly, it seemed, in Maine, would find my mother lying on the lawn with her wrist shattered on a cold October afternoon. The librarian sent me copies of the letters that concerned my father. Letters by him, of him. When I read them, my words left me; I can only say "my blood ran cold."

Nathan need not be troubled with the shenanigans of the fellowship committee, being in Greece and "writing very enthusiastically about the digging," my grandfather writes, while the continent about him is about to burn. And of course Grandfather will pick up the preposterously named Oldfather at the dock in Boston, wearing "a gray hat, light gray top coat, tortoise shell spectacles," and the two, having never met, will continue their discussions of Nathan's future. Oldfather will speak later of his "great pleasure to meet Mrs. Dane and yourself and actually see the kind of home which we could easily enough deduce from Nathan's bearing and personality." Nathan will play tennis, they determine, with and for his impossibly named advisor on Sunday mornings in Urbana, or perhaps "he and Finan could get Saturday hikes and ball-games organized" and with luck, "it would not be long before a few others might acquire the habit of regularity." Oldfather will find his athletic boys the jobs that he deems most appropriate. Father volunteers for a war he will never fight in. He is stationed in New York and takes the train to Columbia to read ancient Greek proverbs in microfilm. There he will doubtless cross paths with my own advisors, whose names he will never know until he reads them with his own on a dedication page

He must have grown to be a man of his time, as men of that time are perceived to be. You've doubtless seen the documentary on the Kennedys, perpetually, it seems, rerun on *American Experience*. I am struck here as I always have been struck by the images of John Kennedy, not the young JFK, now revealed to be so frail, but the jowly president of the very brief early 1960s. I was thirteen. My father was then forty-five. The two images of my father and JFK have coalesced. It is useless, I suppose, to determine whether there is any real resemblance. Yet there they are, Kennedy and my father, in whom I see the same social grace and mannerisms. The graying of the hair and the allusion in the middle-aged frame to a much younger man. Even the old-fashioned sailboats in the background. Perhaps it's just the way a young child sees his father. The smile or the frown. The beaming for the cameras, the contrived look of seriousness.

In a closet somewhere there are some hundred eulogistic notes of sympathy, written at my father's death, addressed to my mother and now saved in shoeboxes. How "he cared about our kids," or "about his students" or "the institution he served so selflessly," and how he "made such a difference." I read these with amazement, for in my adolescent view, he cared little about such things, and drove home obsessively from work each day to the one place he felt safe. I listen again to these multiple voices and I listen for the heart of them. My father, his eulogists, or the mythic Kennedys, authentic Maine, or even Linda Jane herself. I listen for that primary beneath the anecdotes. I want to find that core, but there may well be no core, just the retold stories and revisions. Father's gin bottles still lie empty in the crawl space by the furnace, years after he left them there years after he dramatically quit this habit. Dying, he must have thought, "I need to retrieve those; I will not be embarrassed"; and then he must have thought, "I will not live long enough to be embarrassed." Yet what, I think, poring over the old letters, what if those formal eulogists speak true?

I took up sailing when he died, thinking I, perhaps, could do it right as he had not done it right. With the death of Oldfather, Father's ties to the journals whose names Oldfather recommended in his letters were lost. He settled for becoming not a scholar of Aeschylus but a legendary professor in the college where his father and brother and he had gone and where his kids would go and even briefly teach, and where Oldfather felt it was most appropriate for him to be. I took up sailing. I would thus sail. I would write those books and articles he had left unwritten. I would sail alone, without a needling crew, and I would not be subject to the directives of a distant advisor. This would not be mere playing Maine, but Maine itself. And then I took a job, through no will of mine, on the West Coast and became, finally, one of those much-disparaged summerfolk.

FATHER FALLS FROM THE DINGHY

It is midday in Basin Cove, past noon, the day that Father fell from the dinghy. It has been a morning as I remember most summer mornings to be. Father is once again home and jittery after an early trip to town. But this will be the day he falls from the dinghy.

In those days, he went to town daily in the summer—to do laundry, to buy groceries, to check on a promptly paid bill, to check the mailbox at the Classics Department where he famously taught, to renew an automobile inspection. In all the summers I lived at home, not once was the mailman given a chance to deliver mail to the mailbox, and I'm sure, by 10 AM they just kept the mail out waiting for him. Even Linda Jane had to wait for Father to die in order to leave her barely literate but compelling notes illegally in the mailbox.

Father's behavior embarrassed me. It must have begun some time after his very public renunciation of drinking, and perhaps these imagined tasks were not a product of his nervous obsessions ("He never relaxed. Never," my mother would later say) but a cover to sneak a drink early in the day. He could leave home early in the morning and arrive home only mildly frantic. He could sober up in the afternoon, or so he must have thought, or maybe in the late morning. He would not have to drink himself into oblivion. Sailing in the afternoon must have become part of that routine, and through sailing he could participate in nobler things: the unpredictability of Maine weather, the cycle of the seasons. So he made his journey and imagined his errand and if he hurried through the errand, he would pretend to think, he would be home in time for the perfect wind to come up, which on a presumably perfect day in July or mid-August would be by noon. The breeze would blow at five to fifteen knots from the southwest with no threat of rain or fog. The sea, or what there was of the sea in the Basin, would be calm. He could sail out on the outgoing tide through the narrow gut of what had once been the gristmill at the entrance and sail back through that gut on the incoming tide. He would be home by five, where I would begrudge him a glance from the books I read for graduate school.

I imagine him thinking this, and I am nearly certain he did think it, because longing for alcohol inspires not rationality but the kind of stories he must have told himself. These stories involve both tides and weather conditions. It has taken me years to understand the badness of such thinking, as many years as it has taken me to reconstruct the details of his tortuous reasonings. My brother and I finally cast his ashes in the waters running through the old rock pilings of the gristmill where he spent, I sermon, so much time in life, hung up on the rocks in the falling tide.

Those days he imagined are the perfect sailing days I now never wait for, since such perfectly conforming days can be sailed as all other days can be sailed. There is no reason to feel thwarted by dumb and faceless weather conditions. Weather cannot cheat you; it cannot laugh at you, nor can it play tricks on you or do any of the things that our conventional metaphors make it seem to do. I believe ancient languages have no word for such a thing—weather—and simply give their gods domain over specific conditions, like rain, like the east wind, like the water. Or so I imagine, and so I pronounce, in that logic as clear to me as the logic that ruled my father's summer afternoons was clear to him.

Father's boat, now moored far to the east in an abandoned marina in Eggemoggin Reach, was inconvenient for such serene imaginings: it was small, a catboat, single sail, gaff-rigged, with outsized heavy booms. It must have reminded him of the boats in the old photos of himself and his older brother Duke. It was not a bad sailing boat, as I discovered after he died, but much less handy (oh those heavy booms!) than the smaller, wooden catboat he had owned a few years earlier. Caught in imperfect calm days, the boom would swing idly and viciously past one's skull, and caught in breezy imperfect days, the boom would swing violently and viciously past one's skull. It was a boat he never much loved, and it made his ordinary nervousness unbearable. The worst of the photos of him show him engaged in some routine activity concerning that boat—launching, raising the sail, hauling it out of the water for the winter—things one might in time learn to enjoy, but things he only learned to do. He will have in these photos an absurd scowl, imitating a hard-bitten Mainer in the worst way (or playing one), grim jaw clamped on his cigarette in some preposterous pose of saltiness, and the whole world was now required to shut up and be still and wait its turn until this important task was completed.

Among my sailing photos is one showing my face locked in that same scowl. It was as if he had mischievously willed that look to me. The photo was taken from one of my sailing trips, and when I see it, I feel a sense of embarrassment as intense as the embarrassment a ten-year-old feels, caught smiling, or talking to himself, or looking at the wrong person in the wrong way. The day of that embarrassing photo was the day I thought I had broken my ankle by stepping down into the cabin while heroically holding a plate of spaghetti. And I see in the photo that same studied fatigue (so contrived!), as if sailing in Maine were the grimmest, most taxing thing the universe could assign, and you, so tough and salty, just endured it, telling the world to shut the hell up and wait its turn.

When I saw that expression, I vowed never to let myself feel that way again, and particularly never to feel that way on a boat again. There is nothing grim about sailing or loving or anything else you do for pleasure. If you sail alone, there is no crew to get injured, no child to cry, no one to get uncomfortable or bored; and if you are truly alone, there is no one to disappoint onshore. The world turns in its irrevocable formulae and the ocean moves in its indeterminate course, and you move and there is nothing to be grim and lockjawed about. It is all just spaghetti in an unwashed plastic plate.

But this is about Father and the dinghy, not about what I inherited from him.

It was one of the perfect days he waited for, but it would, in his mind, be spoiled by noontime guests. There must be something wrong with my memory here. I cannot remember whose guests they would be. It must have been a ladies' lunch with friends of my mother. Father thus had his presumably unwanted audience and so—stoically, in the all too brief hours between his pressing morning duties—laundry? mail? groceries?—in the brief hours between those duties and the social necessity of saying goodbye to guests, he would sail, he thought, and the newly arrived guests (or was it workmen?) would see him majestically row the dinghy out, lost in his own world he would be thought, and doing what he was thought to love, without a thought of anything else like lunch guests (or was it really workmen?). It is as if the things that we are thought to love are witnessed; as if our very solitude were watched. And if you think that way, as my father did, you will, as he did, come to a series of bad ends.

I think of these years as the years Linda Jane became the "postperson," it being the beginning of the "person" period in American vocabulary that summer in the 1980s. She worked in one of the local grocery stores or package stores and on her break she would sometimes bring the mail to me. But they aren't quite the same years at all. I never sailed with Father or sailed at all when he was alive, and Linda Jane and I lusted out on the water somewhere long after Father died and long after I took up his purported love of sailing. She was nearly deaf and when she spoke, she took a quick breath first as if finding the words, and her sentences were always clipped and punctuated with nods as she gulped for further words and phrases. I could not whisper lewd suggestions to her in public, because she had too little sense of irony to understand, and would not have heard them in any case, even with her new hearing aid. You cannot, and could not even then, walk the cobblestones of

Portland shouting lewdness in your lover's deaf ears. But she drove me, I would say, falling back on the worst of clichés, to distraction, and though I could not speak to her (can this be true?), she loved me, and used to say that as best she could in doubtlessly misspelled platitudes composed with her calloused hands on my back as she lay next to me. They are the messages I could pretend not to understand as she pretended not to hear when her lover's wit got too tangled for her. Just her hand against my back and her shoulder against my hip while we sailed and she sat next to the tiller.

Linda Jane never saw my father, never met him, and never suffered his lascivious glance at her boyish form. She is now lying with me on the floor of the downstairs room of the guesthouse. She is wearing the gray sweater she wore on cool summer evenings. She is looking at me, and we are making up for lost time. We are making up for the failed weekend rendezvous a week earlier, when I cut short a weeklong trip to New York so I could return home to debauch her. I arrive hotly home; my mother ridiculously insists I have cut short that week in New York to see my ineptly visiting sister.

We were always missing such moments: the weather was bad; panting rivals hounded us with flowers; babysitters were right booked up. We drove too far from home one night and found ourselves rattling around in her oversized car through the dark fields where she once learned to play at love (I guessed) in high school. The faces of surprised young lovers stare at us in amazement from the cars parked in the dark and unused roadway.

I knock on her door. Her parents are there to watch the sunset. Retired, they now have nothing better to do, I think. "I told them I had plans," she says, but they remain. She turns into my driveway and finds part of my family vacationing in the guesthouse. On the last day in September, she brings the mail to my door, and as she hugs me I let myself feel the curve of her back. Then she said goodbye, and the next day I left for California. Two years later, past now lying in the chop at the mooring, and past rounding the red buoy, and past even tacking about by Drunker Ledge and lying in bed while she misspells her phrases on my back, it is too late. She is busy; she is not at home, unfindable, at work, away. A friend, told all this, explains what is obvious to all but me: she no longer wants to see or wait for me.

So Linda Jane is gone now, to Idaho, or Texas, or Arizona, and there is no one at the old grocery store to ask after her, and Mother cannot innocently inquire for her at the hairdresser's, since Mother, too, is gone, nor are ex-husbands and ex-friends of much use in this matter. Her parents finally die as well, as they all do, one by one. I find her listed as the survivor and I wonder, if I were to call, if she would answer, if she could hear me. Would she still know that she was Linda Jane at all? But the call I make is only this one, recounting the chance. And Linda Jane, I suppose, is back in Idaho.

All Father wanted was to be a regular joe, a regular guy. So he wore jeans when it was not yet right for the bourgeoisie and swore with a studied Maine accent, also then more retrograde than fashionable. He did Maine things like paint boats and houses, and made an attempt to garden, and tried to fish and run borrowed equipment, and talked of retiring and just lobstering or gardening or something regular and ordinary like that. But regular guys were not as he was, bred and led by his controlling mother and dressed up as an Eagle Scout all proud beside her in the old photo graph. He went to war but, unlike regular guys, didn't fight, and his war stores were boring and unviolent, as the stories of regular guys were not, since they, the real fighters, never told stories at all if they lived that long. And he, so irregular, outdid himself as he wrote neo-Housmanian poems (of course) and played tennis in the same whites in which my awful grandmother dressed him so she could pose with him, beaming, in the old photos.

For a man as nervous and self-agitated as he was, Father had moments of absolute clarity and calm. One of these was when he was studying a particularly complex Greek verb. All those voices, moods, and tenses! Who requires such niceties? Another was when he was aiming a firearm, a great paradox for a man as utterly timid and pacifistic as he was, as hyperactive and obsessive. I never saw him miss a shot, except when he lost his mind briefly and went for the rat on the suet feeder, leaving a pattern of birdshot on the house siding. His weapon was a shotgun, a single-shot .410, a load so light it cannot legally I think be used to hunt. He prided himself on the inadequacy of equipment, like the plywood dinghy he once sailed in the bay until its seams gave out and it rotted as a garden ornament. His victims were generally woodchucks, hit at the outermost limits of the range. I share none of this skill with him. My woods are full of always-invisible game, and my ears ring unpleasantly from sightings-in on makeshift firing ranges. I leave the woodchucks alone.

Despite the occasional public buffoonery he was known for, there was a certain desperation to all that Father did. All, that is, except public speaking, which for some reason did not terrify or intimidate him. And when the coaches called him halfway through the sports awards dinner because I had forgotten to tell him I had promised him as a speaker that night, he wrote the witty speech in his head as he drove in, tying the Windsor one-handed as he did. "A poor man's Herbie Brown," he styled himself, in a now-abstruse allusion to a then notoriously orotund colleague at Bowdoin.

He was also an amateur ornithologist. He recorded his bird sightings in a loose-leaf, always structurally evolving, notebook, and kept lists, lists, and sought out rare species, and browsed through flocks of ducks on cold January mornings, and identified even the most bewildering of fall warblers. As a child, I had none of this patience, but preferred to look at the flock in the distance, listen to his discoursing, and, on the theory that I had indeed "seen" what he identified—somewhere out there—enter that species in my more rationally constructed birdbook.

One of the rarest and most spectacular winter birds one will find in his birdbook is the northern shrike, a small, jay-like, predatory bird that is rumored, perhaps correctly, to prey on chickadees and nuthatches and small rodents and pin its prey on the thorns of hawthorn trees. I never saw such things. But at ten years old, I was awed by the lamentations of Father and the neighbors, all serious ornithologists, over the terror of "their" chickadees (birds as common as the seed that lured them to the window feeders) as they froze in fear in the lilac trees. Shrikes, apparently, were more familiar to chickadees than to near-expert ornithologists. Among these ornithologists, there was none of the enthusiasm over the rarity of the thing one might expect—none of the frantic phone calls and car trips consequent on the discovery of the scissor-tailed flycatcher in a neighboring field a year earlier—that, too, recorded in my own book, since in the field I looked in the direction where it was said to be, and surely "saw" everything that flew about there. And after a series of frantic telephone calls about the shrike threatening the winter bird feeders, Father took the .410 out and, from a distance of thirty yards, always on the limit of the range, shot the shrike, a far rarer thing than any flycatcher, off the top of the apple tree and let me bury it, now fully seen, in a shoebox next to the shed. Had I kept this incident in mind, I would never have let him take my aging dog to the vet the year both of them died. There was something I call murderous about Father's generosity and gentility. When my dog got old and was vet-bound, Father spared me, he claimed, that common experience of putting dogs down, and gave me an uncommon one. He took the dog for what was to be a routine check and had the dog killed for me. And when he returned and I was in shock at what he had done, Mother told me it would be unseemly to confront him.

Father rowed the dinghy out and maybe now I remember more clearly when it was. I was still working on the fishing boat, and consequently I felt a peculiar competence about the water—that competence fishermen have that is related to the fact that most of them, absurdly, cannot swim. Swimming is not something fishermen need to know, because it is something they simply must not have to do. Falling into the water, for a fisherman, is entirely out of the question.

Father rowed the dinghy out, and there was something odd about the way my mother (waiting for her guests) told me to check on him. Something detached, like the way she told me not to break down and cry in front of him when he was dying of cancer and I knew I would never see him again. Like that. So I walked down to the shore, all salty, tanned, young, and muscular, I thought, thinking of Linda Jane, and I saw him there, or his head there, spitting angrily with his arm over the cheap plastic dinghy and drifting with the tide to shore. "You need help?" Just his head, still wearing somehow the inappropriate captain's hat I see him wear in all the photos and floating away from the mooring with his son and God knows how many lunch guests watching the whole damn thing. When I realized he wouldn't drown, I laughed (or pretended to), as if both of us were so competent we found this breach of competence merely amusing, which neither of us did.

And then there is nothing. I remember nothing. No sputtering as he came ashore. No dragging the light dinghy over the seaweed and dumping the water out. No changing into dry clothes. No elaborate and embarrassed curses. It is as if the story ended and there was nothing but ignominy and I have done him the favor of forgetting it. For I was not particularly young and muscular in those days, because I was neither working on the lobster boat nor sailing, nor was I thinking of Linda Jane. I was, rather, reading old books in libraries somewhere and spending my summers at home. The only thing that remains to trigger and define this memory is the wide and heavy dinghy I now own and inherited from him. So wide and heavy is this boat that it charts my slow decline in strength each fall when I try to haul it over the bank for the winter. So stable is this dinghy, you can swim right up to it and haul yourself over the side rail. And as you flop onto the floorboards, you will hear him as he floats past in his captain's hat, angrily cursing with the outgoing tide.

CHAPTER FIVE

POTTS HARBOR

O what excuse will my poor beast then find,
When swift extremity can seem but slow?

—Shakespeare

CRUISING GUIDES

Roger Duncan's *A Cruising Guide to the New England Coast* was first published in 1937, the same year my father graduated from Bowdoin; it has been reedited and reprinted many times. For decades, this was the only alternative to the laconic notes in the *United States Coast Pilot,* and most boats that cruise Maine today carry a copy in one of its many editions. You can also find copies on the bookshelves of nearly any turn-of-the-century cottage on the Maine coast, and by "turn of the century" I refer of course to the last century. For sailors, there are far more useful and more recent guides available: Hank and Jan Taft's *A Cruising Guide to the Maine Coast* (now revised), and Don Johnson's *Cruising Guide to Maine* (itself revised), the best of all of them. But you're less likely to find these in the shingled cottages. Duncan established the form and tone of these books, and perhaps because it really isn't about sailing at all, his book will prove to be the most tenacious.

A guide of any kind is written under a false premise, what a scholar calls "full presence of the truth." All is known, or supposedly known, although no one really knows the Maine past or the Maine coast all that well. Every scholar and every teacher I have met fears the same thing: "One day, *they will find out*"—that terrifying *they* of peer reviewers or deans or school principals or referees of journals or one's own students, and they will shake their heads in unison and mutter, "Fraud." I have no doubt that Duncan and the Tafts, the astonishingly competent Johnson, and even the anonymous authors of the *United States Coast Pilot* fear the same thing: that one day, sailors will realize they know nothing of the winds and tides and currents; that one day, as they maneuver toward a dock, an old harbormaster will turn away in contempt. Thus, in scholarly books, the impenetrable footnotes; and thus, in the guides and in the language of sailing magazines, the anecdotes, the jargon, and the accents of false modesty.

Of all the voices in these guides, Duncan's is the most memorable but also the most evasive. It is difficult to say exactly who or what this Duncan is: you look at the inside cover of his books in the shingled Maine cottages and you will find a string of dates: revisions, reprintings, reeditings. In the book itself, the sentences you read could belong to any one of them.

We are now used to this and seem to accept it: this incompletion, technicians out there fiddling, adding entries, revising old entries, deleting others. Mistakes can be corrected, remade, left to be corrected. Our reference books and guides no longer stay in place. They change, the way we hope our seascapes will not change; they outgrow their errors; they introduce new ones. The Duncan book, the edition I own, now quite battered from being thrown from its shelf as the boat heels, is dated 1979, the year I took up sailing. But Duncan must have been long dead by then. And many of Duncan's revisers are now dead as well.

The Duncan language I find most disturbing is found, I think, in an edition from the 1930s. Duncan speaks:

> A story is told of a distinguished Harvard professor, long a summer resident of North Haven. Two fishermen were watching him sail a small boat in the Thorofare. The professor was having a good deal of trouble keeping clear of anchored yachts. Said one to the other, "Old Professor—*knows* an awful lot, but he don't *re-a-lize* nothin'."

This is not a joke, because it isn't really funny. It is a moral tale of sorts, with academics like myself the butt of it. But Duncan's phrases capture neither the inflections of the fishermen nor the realities in which they live: by the time the revision I own went to press, commercial fishermen could not and, likely as a point of pride, would not sail.

The most unsettling character in Duncan is President
Eliot, of course from Harvard, as is the professor in the
above anecdote. Here is Eliot, as characterized by a voice
described only as that of a "correspondent": "There is a crop
of interesting stories about President Eliot, who, as you
may know, was a very skillful sailor . . ." We know these anecdotes are reputable because they come from "the late M.
W. Rodman Peabody of Boston, son of Dr. Peabody . . ."
Again: "I shall always remember another fresh southwest
afternoon . . . the President had gone cruising with us as far
east as Cutler . . ."

Where is Duncan in all this? The following is from the
edition of the 1960s; I believe this is Duncan's own voice,
but I am not certain of that:

> We are strongly prejudiced in favor of the people who
> live in coastal communities the year round . . . Local
> people . . . still have a characteristic manner of
> speech, still use colloquialisms that we consider pic-
> turesque . . . still dress in a way different from ours.
> Most . . . have poured more salt water out of their
> boots than we have ever sailed over . . . If a fisherman
> gives you advice, take it and thank him. If he helps
> you in a difficult crisis, thank him and offer him a
> drink in the cockpit.

I read this thinking of the boat gear I left unlocked in my
yard over the winter, missing now. I feel the knife held to my
throat by a trusted fisherman I once worked for. I hear the

belligerent rants of another. The thought of inviting such men to drink in a confined and overly refined cockpit is only part of what disturbs me as I read this passage.

Duncan and his revisers transcend, or they themselves might say "lie athwart" these two cultures, the culture of "local people" versus "the gregarious, the inexperienced navigators, and those who like to dress up and go ashore for dinner at the yacht club." They feign contempt for one while condescending to the other. They live in a society filled with his Doctors and Professors and Presidents of Harvard, and that would-be aristocracy of stalwart Americans who claim to have "worked for it." They relate as brothers to the local fishermen who are themselves strangely and obtusely locked in the economics of the late last century. Duncan's admonitions flatter us, defining the company we true sailors keep—not a doctor from Belfast, but from Boston, and not a history teacher from Farmington, but the President of Harvard.

In the 1930s, one might feel a genuine nostalgia for this mythical state of things. There was, in the late nineteenth century, a brief peace or so they thought, and New Englanders and their taciturn fishermen looked forward both to a time of peace prior to World War I just as they did prior to World War II, and, yes, in this view of history, things might last this way forever. Those were days of love and hate, I guess, when the words caught in the trees and mastheads and just stuck there; when it rained so dense, the back-winded sea blew flat.

Before the automobile changed this Edenic state of things, the families came up by steamer, and those without the luxury of tickets and homes in Massachusetts endured the winters in picturesque misery. You can see the steamer landings in the collections of postcards you will find in antiques shops up and down the coast. There are a few remnant pilings on the shore of Potts Harbor itself, but you need the postcards to know where to look for them. Sarah Orne Jewett wrote best about that time because she had none of the sentimentality of those who later looked back at it. None of the contrived manner of speech found in Duncan's characters or in the way my father spoke, imitating the way my grandfather spoke, who, though he lived in Lexington and worked in some thankless job for Hood Rubber Co., could still say "a-yuh" without irony. Listen in Jewett to the embarrassed Captain Bowden apologize for his landing:

"I'm beat if I ain't aground after all!" mourned the captain despondently.

But I could reach the bowsprit, and he pushed with the boat-hook, while the wind veered round a little as if on purpose and helped with the sail; so presently the boat was free and began to drift out from shore.

"Used to call this p'int Joanna's wharf privilege, but 't has worn away in the weather since her time. I thought one or two bumps wouldn't hurt us none,— paint's got to be renewed, anyway,—but I never thought she'd tetch. I figured on shyin' by," the captain apologized. "She's too gre't a boat to handle well in here; but I used to sort of shy by in Joanna's day, an' cast a little somethin' ashore—some apples or a couple o' pears if I had 'em—on the grass, where she'd be sure to see."

This is, I call it, playing Maine for real.

UNDER WAY

Despite jokes about its variability, the general state of Maine weather is quite stable from year to year, controlled as it is by the Labrador current, formed from the ice melting from the polar ice cap. I expect this weather to persist through my lifetime until the last ice melts and catastrophe ensues. In mid-June, the so-called Bermuda high that produces the warm southwesterly airflow later in the summer has not yet "set up." Consequently there is fog; there is rain; there is sun; and on most days, you will contend with cold. In mid-June, schools are still in session. Many marinas are still closed. Anchorages are wide open. Cruising boats and even weekday sailors are rare. A few fishermen are working, and for some, it is the end of the winter season. If you leave from the well-protected Potts Harbor at this time, you will sail easily east, retaining these still-lingering spring conditions, and when you return, you will sail west into the approaching summer.

The guides say little about this special time of year, and I discovered this perfect season quite by accident. One day, by chance, I lost Linda Jane for the last time. And when by chance I lost Linda Jane for good, I went sailing, and I've been reenacting that June ever since.

I did not lose her easily, because, for Linda Jane, nothing was easy or simple. I had left her in California, where I assumed she would spend the summer with her husband, but then I heard she had miraculously gotten a job in Los Angeles and quit her somewhat less miraculously obtained job in Nebraska at a time no one but the most skilled or fortunate got jobs. She would leave the Nebraska plains where I had found her and return to California and then I guess I myself would return to Los Angeles to be with her forever, or so the story must have gone in someone's version of it.

Losing Linda Jane was intricate, like one of those astonishing constructions in *The Ashley Book of Knots*. It begins with a rumor that some friend or maybe former student of mine had also gotten a job in Nebraska at a time when none but the miraculously skilled or fortunate got jobs. Hadn't this same man, I recalled, sat on the aluminum-framed chair in my living room for a half hour, extolling the virtues of Linda Jane, saying how he would helplessly, he claimed, fall in love with her? And hadn't I, wittily I thought, as in the movies, hadn't I told him that he was the only human being besides her husband who did not know we were having a passionate affair and had been involved for years? So when I heard that both he and Linda Jane had miraculously found jobs in the plains of America, and then had left the plains of America for the urbanity of California and just as miraculously found a second pair of jobs there, all these miracles during the precise time our passionate affair seemed to be in abeyance, I knew it was time to call Linda Jane and have what would doubtless be our last conversation.

Linda Jane was steadfast even in the smallest of things. She styled herself an ardent supporter of the institution of marriage, and claimed it was cynical and cold of me not to commit to her before she divorced her husband. She accused me of infidelities, and when I parried with her own relation to her husband, she claimed that didn't count, even though I was never sure which of us I was characterizing as a victim. When I assured her of my own recent and inadvertent faithfulness, she claimed that did not count either, because there was that small matter of Linda Jane delivering the mail or was it the French guitarist or a tall and sturdy Teutonic Linda Jane shaking her head in apologies and saying alas, she was just monogamous (the word did not come easily in her Teutonic lexicon) and one more time and that would be the end of it. Why, I thought, had I ever revealed these small irrelevancies?

The telephone call is as follows, a transcription, not a memory: "I hear you have a job." "Yes." "In Los Angeles?" "Yes." "And G., I hear he has a job there too." "Yes." "And are you moving there?" "Yes, next week." "And G., is he moving there as well?" "Yes." "Same address?" . . . And that is how I began my sailing trips.

INJURIES

It is difficult to begin. There are losses and things one forgets and bad weather conditions. The calendar is never quite right, the numbers all on the wrong days, and people waiting, inconveniently, for your return. And my arm, my heart—these fail as well.

I have never been seriously injured. To be seriously injured involves pain and nights in hospitals; it means having a moral story to tell that will either chart the heroics of injury, the injustice of it, or the philosophical implications of the randomness in the universe. And so I have never been seriously injured nor imagined it in any coherent way. Yet I have often begun my sailing trips with infirmities.

It is June. I am to leave the next day. I go for an evening jog, and I laugh thinking of Linda Jane many years earlier and the logic that tormented her as much as it baffled me. Mother is asleep, or nearly so, watching television, or maybe in those years she is still able to read. The cool air is perfect for jogging in early June in the evening; the colors are beginning to brighten. You cannot avoid the mist in the air, the softening of the lines between the land and the sky and the water. It is cool enough that most locals stay inside to eat and watch the evening news. You run with no impediment but the illusory wind you yourself create. I come home, thinking of the cool and moist June air, and the weather predicted for the next morning, and the food in the bottom of the refrigerator that one year I accidentally left behind. I drink a glass of water and urinate a cup of blood into my recently repaired toilet.

These were not flecks of blood. But pure, thick, crimson blood. Like wounds in the movies. Like opening a vein. Like cutting yourself shaving. Like menstruating. Like cuts on the face and skull that bleed profusely and laughably with even the most minimal of injuries. Like the cut on one's hand in the fall when it is so cold in the woods you have no feeling but the cool blood running down your fingers onto the grip of the Winchester. I stop. I wait. I urinate again. The sentence I form then is: "There must be some mistake." But what mistake? What order of mistake? A dream? There would have been more to a dream—two penises, a crowd of onlookers. Was there some method in urination that I had forgotten? Do we all, untrained, bleed this way? What kind of forgetting? What kind of medical mishap could this be? Had I forgotten about seeing blood so thick? So close? Was there nothing unusual about this? Was this the meaning of the private stalls in public restrooms?

"Don't, uh, ur'nate in a public washroom after taking that," the young but wholesome girl in the Nebraska drugstore had blessedly once warned me.

I began to think. The boat is packed for the trip. I plan to leave in the morning. My alarmingly healthy but aging mother must not be disturbed; I had not disturbed her in fifty years. I must remember to take the groceries from the bottom of the refrigerator. Would there be ice in the ice machine on the wharf? Would I leave anything essential behind? Were there batteries? Alcohol for the stove? Would it rain? Were the Red Sox on a West Coast trip? I ran to the car. On the way, I invented an excuse for Mother, something about missing groceries or chandlery or the like. "I forgot some food; I need a two-inch galvanized bell shackle." I distinctly remember the word "galvanized." She did not answer. She did not know what a shackle was or what it was or was not good for. She did not seem curious. She did not seem surprised or suspicious. But there was nothing that I said in the nearly sixty years I spoke with my mother that made her look suspicious.

The car started. I put it in gear and backed around in the driveway. The same car is in my driveway today, its once-faded paint faded more. My bladder is full of blood, thick, cinematic blood. When I look at my lap, will it be full of blood? I drove fifteen miles to the emergency room, now thinking more clearly, now thinking, yes, this is Life; and that was Life, and now Life is dealing with this life of internal bleeding. I thought this, I remember, as I was passing the next hill past the house that Linda Jane would own in a decade. Life is thus an adventure, as in the original meaning of "that which comes to you—the advent of one's new life." It is like leaving on a sailing trip; it is like the bad news one has never imagined. I believe I was only parroting things seen in the movies, or perhaps in an interview in the *LA Weekly* with a cancer patient who describes his diagnosis as a great relief, as the road rolls quietly beneath the car still parked in my driveway today. I have blood in my urine.

Therefore I am bleeding. I am bleeding, but I am strangely uninjured.

The nurse in the emergency room was less unsettled than I. She was a nurse and a professional and had seen everything there was to see, even in the small, unpressured emergency rooms of hospitals in southern Maine. She was used to calming hysterical patients, particularly male patients who proved to be less tough than the males they watch on television. I knew all this before I saw her. I knew all this. Everything had always been fine in my life and everything would continue to be fine. It was the kind of bland life anyone would be happy to live. The nurse was or would be a woman; she would not be in the least bit squeamish about blood, no matter what its source. Does Linda Jane herself not talk of packing wounds of accident victims in the county hospital of Los Angeles without a trace of sentiment or emotion? She is the reason one goes to the emergency room. "It's all right," she says, or would say. "Don't worry. You men are such babies. A little blood is nothing, as all women who menstruate know. It flows through your veins and out of your veins, and life goes on. It supplies you with oxygen. Those who imagine you breathe to gather oxygen are mistaken. It is the blood that provides. Always the blood. Here, fill this cup." Maybe what she actually said was: "I'm sure it's fine; just fill this cup." She is the reason governments support nursing schools: there are men, real men, with blood flowing from rather than into their sexual organs, and society needs professionals who can calm them. "You men!" We are all such boys at heart. What do we know of blood?

I fill my cup. It is again as if I had opened a vein. That thick staged blood of the bad detective shows. The Kubrick-esque blood of the war movies. I have seen it pulled from my arm into a clear syringe as I give blood samples always proving I am in perfect health. I have seen it splatter on the sidewalk after the lid of my station wagon hit me as I tried to get an angry and hysterical Linda Jane to the airport. But it is only that. Blood. What flows through one's veins. I am assured now. Confident. We men indeed! And now, girl-like, completely at one with my body, I gratefully hand the sample to my nurse, she too as confident and calm and professionally bored as unseen pilots in cockpits. Calmly, she glances at the cup. "Jesus Christ!" she screams in panic. "Is this *yours?!*"

Years later, I have another trip planned. I will leave on Tuesday. On the weekend before, I drive to what is called Upcountry—Greenville, Dixmont, Oneonta, Brownville Junction—I do not know what these places are, nor the origin of their names. I only know that my wife came from that region and now my aging hippie friends own camps there that to the undiscerning eye are little distinguishable from the modest but grid-dependent houses they call their permanent homes.

When I arrived at the top of their newly constructed gravel driveway, I drove my still-familiar car straight through that soft gravel into the newly created ditch, where it hung precariously immobile. And all my friends put on their best Maine accents and, hippie and masculine, shooed me aside as they winched my car from their marvelous ditch with the curious machinery they have attached to their front bumpers for occasions, I imagine, just like this one.

I stood aside with the women. We swam. They worked on carpentry. We paddled; they worked on ditches. We talked about the sunfish that had attacked John's private parts a year earlier and drawn blood. John is now gone, and I tell the story in his place every chance I get, even though all who hear have heard the story and my version many times before. I will tell how John rests naked in the water, watching the ridiculous sunfish hovering between his legs with uncommon interest. I will demonstrate the matching movement of fish and flesh with my open hand. The fish attacks. The men, though hippies to the core, swim in swimsuits as a consequence. "Safety's on," I hear them say.

I drove home on Monday, thinking of the wives of the working men and planning to leave the next morning. But Monday night was a difficult night, and the symptoms of my condition are well-known ones: shortness of breath, tightness in the chest, pain radiating down one arm, sweats. This too I had seen on TV, or read about in interviews with the sick. I had studied the warnings, and the trailers for the weekly hospital dramas. It is as insensitive to make light of this as it is to treat a cupful of blood in a urine sample as a source of amusement. I called the emergency room in the morning, wondering what to do, hoping I would find that reassuring Linda Jane of my imagination (Don't worry! You men!) rather than the real one shouting, "*Yours?* Jesus Christ, is this *yours?!*" You men. Go sailing. This is nothing.

So sure was I, and so foolish having decided to drive to town in the first place, that I mistook the pause on the other end of the phone for just that nurse, shaking her head. "You men. Pain radiating down the arm? We have the genuinely sick and infirm to deal with. Stay home." "Should I bother to come in?" I asked, having explained my symptoms. Again that pause. "Sir, you must understand," said the unexpectedly male voice. "Normally, when we get a call like this, the first question we ask is, 'Where do we send the ambulance?'" "Thanks. I believe that answers my question."

I drove. If I died on the way, it would not matter whether I died of a heart attack or in an accident. I would feel the pain like lost love, and then it would be gone and nothing would matter. Again, thinking my thoughts of Life . . . that was Life and now this is Life and life . . . the same familiar thoughts I had rehearsed years before in the familiar car, thinking of my blood in the plastic cup. And perhaps it would end that way too, with the young doctor shaking his head saying, "Probably nothing. Maybe a kidney. If it's that, you have months before you need to do anything. Go sailing. Pee to leeward, and have it checked out when you get to Los Angeles."

And I learned an important maxim about emergency rooms in small towns or even large cities. To your broken hand, or, say, blood in your urine, be sure to add: "and oh yes, some trouble breathing, and some chest pain, radiating down one arm, in fact, directly to this hangnail you may as well look at in passing." In the emergency room that early morning, all other patients were wheeled aside—the old lady after night-long pain and hysterics, the whimpering child with the early morning broken limb, the young couple brought in from the mythical drive-in still hooked together like dogs. I was given machines and a young doctor who ignored all those other patients and kept asking about those hippies on the weekend. Just what did you do? As relentlessly as he probed, I parried: no, no drugs, too old, no wild thrashings, too staid . . . About that weekend . . . No drugs, no grand philandering, just canoeing. Still on the machine with the readouts. Really. "You do much canoeing?" Or was it, "Ever do any canoeing at all?" Or, "Doesn't that require a lot of upper-arm movement, say, overuse of the muscles in the chest, to which you are not accustomed, and perhaps cause a lot of fatigue?"

Linda Jane would call this ACS: acute canoeing syndrome. And yes, I went sailing, and didn't forget the food in the bottom of the refrigerator, and that time, I did not have to remind myself to aim to leeward.

Then it is spring again, last spring; I have decided to fix Linda Jane's window the day before sailing. This is the house I passed years earlier on the way to the emergency room. This time, I trip on the shrub branches she has trimmed and hit both shins on the brick landing to the front door she never uses. And two days into sailing I took off my sailing pants and saw my leg misshapen and black and blue from the knee to the heel. On some sea, was it, I had sprained that ankle I suppose somewhere during the north- west wind and perhaps the pain of the shin had been too great to notice. Or maybe my leg was broken and maybe it wasn't. And perhaps I would have another story about a strange emergency room.

And then I am back in California. Linda Jane, recently arrived from England, is about to leave me for good on her way to a fellowship at the Folger in Washington. She has no truck with sailing at all; no, Linda Jane is all about seventeenth-century English history plays and doesn't give, as she claimed imitating a Maine vulgarity, a "rat's ass" about sailing. I opened the station wagon hatch (the bon- net, as the Brits call it). The pistons that hold the hatch open were weak, I suppose, and then I was on all fours in the driveway staring at the pool of blood directly under my head that grew and grew and grew as my Folger-bound scholar of English plays stood by screaming as for some reason I hand her the keys to the apartment.

If you are so injured, I found, and fearful of the emer- gency room, take Linda Jane instead to LAX. Warn her maybe that if you see double or begin vomiting uncontrol- lably, you will have to stop and she can then take a taxi, be- cause Linda Jane may well be a very poor driver and very concerned about missing that plane. Walk into LAX with Linda Jane's luggage in one hand and a towel held to your head with the other and your shirt soaked in blood. Within seconds, you will have two EMTs and their supervisor crowded around you, cleaning, bandaging, advising, questioning, worrying that you will sue, and asking something ridiculous about whether you are able to be aroused, and even Linda Jane will laugh at that.

The next morning, my landlady, who lived below me, called in concern; she had noticed the trail of blood leading up the steps to the door; she said nothing about my loud cries for help on the quiet street outside her door at 10 PM. I told the story. She listened. She had rented me this apartment in Venice, the perfect apartment in Venice. I claimed for years I would leave it only for full-time living in Maine or in a box. And although she was a bit New Age, and unfit for my taste, when she took her lover's cigar that day on the street corner and drew deeply she came suddenly to life. She listened. I assured her I was fine. "Oh wonderful," she said. "This is probably also a great time to bring this up. I've been planning to evict you and move into your wonderful apartment for the last two years at my convenience, and now that all is set, you have thirty days. Have a great day." It was the last day I would truly live on the Pacific.

Lesser injuries than these are a constant on boats, at least on mine. The cabin is small. If you stretch, you hit your hand against the intricately designed brass latches on the porthole. If you stand suddenly, your head grazes the teak border of the hatchway, and if you are wearing well-heeled boots you hit your head there. Sometimes the Velcro-stripped mosquito netting merely snatches your hat off.

Even your habits can be dangerous. When you step up out of the cabin, you learn to use the handholds and look straight ahead to where you will step to assess the situation in the cockpit. You do this without thinking. If you forget you have earlier closed the hatch, you will raise yourself hard into it. It is possible to give yourself a concussion, and Charlie was nearly knocked senseless in this manner.

Anywhere on the boat, if you lose balance and you always do, you will catch yourself on your knees and shins and you will slowly build up a series of unidentified bruises on your lower leg, like those inflicted by the brick landing of Linda Jane's front door. When you do not clearly identify the flickering alcohol flame from the stove, you will lose the hair on your forearm; you may ignite or melt your down jacket. Every step is a potential and ignominious misstep. It is hard to plan around them.

For years, I drove for five days west each August to Los Angeles. Wary of the great desert in eastern California on the last day west, I would dawdle for the morning in Grants, New Mexico, leaving at 10 AM so I could cross the desert after the cooling sunset and still arrive home at my ideal but doomed Venice apartment by midnight. And thinking that, I know that all these staccato stories of real and imagined injuries—these too are mere delays.

Sometimes it is simply best to go.

CHAPTER SIX

FISHING ON CASCO BAY

This winged voyager, how weak he is, out of his
*   element,*
Once so beautiful, how comic and ugly.
A sailor pokes a pipe into his beak,
Another limps, mocking this sick bird of the sky.
                    —Baudelaire, "The Albatross"

It was on the east side of Harpswell that the real injury took place, one that marks another beginning of the life I now have on the water and the end of my working life on the water. This is the injury that matters, not the ones I tell these stories of. And it is not these minor things I suffered on my own boat or when I worked on the fishing boat: not the bad back or the cuts and running sores on my hands, nor the indelible sunburn on my arm, or the summers of lost sleep. It is David's injury, which I think claimed him shortly after my father died; David, lobstering finally without me, days after holding the knife to my throat and smiling all those impotent belligerencies, those threats so common among fishermen, who, with unprotected gear strewn out on the water, cannot risk the violence and destruction such threats imply. Once more and predictably David had gotten drunk at a party; he drove his motorcycle into a litigious partygoer, and there he lost his foot and much of his mind and wasted his kids' inheritance on lawyers.

I was told of this injury by my in-law, fishing out of Gurnet, also on the east side of Harpswell. I was relieved. He was dead and not yet dead. There was no telling, in that brief informative phone call, how much longer I would feel bound to endure the knife held to my throat, or whether those evenings were finally gone for good.

When I visited him in the hospital, he was lunatic, but his lunacy was directed, such that the one person he was addressing could understand it. He talked to me of fishing, the bad bait from Nova Scotia, hauling back, but John, who was with me, followed none of this; then he turned to John and suddenly I understood nothing, and John laughed and said, wrongly as it turned out, all would one day be fine. But how could this turn out fine? And what would be the point of returning him to the knife-wielding belligerence of a week ago?

A few days later, the nurses (still those nurses) said on the phone he was much improved. No raving. I drove to the hospital. For twenty minutes I listened to him ramble, listened to what his now keepers called improvement. I realized he didn't know me. He had known me a week earlier, but no more. There was nothing about fishing here. Nothing of our days on the water. And I swore to and at him that if he continued to manipulate me that way I would never deal with him again. And he smiled a mock cherubic smile and I kept that unhealthy promise until the end, recalling him only in the elaborate curses I construct when something goes wrong sailing.

He was a much different man years earlier, when I was different and nineteen and didn't know a thing about boats or work or anything of the sort. I answered an ad for summer work: the laconic "Lobstering—$100/week" which sounded far better than working in a shoe shop, or delivering chickens door-to-door, or playing in bad bands, or watching unseen kids astride dogfish in the late afternoon, so I answered that ad, and life changed for me.

I learned to tie bowlines, and fisherman's knots, and half hitches, and how to secure the skiff's painter to an outhaul. I learned about selecting bait, and weighing hundred-pound crates of lobsters, and slowing my pace just enough so that David would help me move the 350-pound bait barrels. I learned about intimidation, and how to do that by saying nothing, and how to keep and lose one's temper, and also how to drive drunk at midday at the end of a week's work.

All this occurred on Casco Bay, that place where, bound east, the Maine coast changes from the lazy spread of beaches to the rockbound coast of the vacation photographs. In Casco Bay, those unique ridges of rock pushed up from plates or volcanoes now lie in long ridges oriented north-south, the greatest of them the two main peninsulas themselves. Each island, each ledge, and, as I discovered while working on that boat, each underwater ravine where the lobsters (fish, as we called them) moved in midseason— all lie north-south. I can still find those regularities on the modern depth-sounder, and following those ridges and ravines, I can still see him. He is still there, as if locked in the readouts of the screen, adrift in the underwater ridges and ravines themselves, though dead now and before that, years from remembering anything about it all, there he is, yaw-balanced in the following sea, howling those strange and awful verses of Gerard Manley Hopkins, as we worked, and the bent warp, as I wrote once, lay on the floorboards.

WORDS AND THINGS

Ashore, rope is rope; on a boat, it is line. The front and back of the boat are bow and stern. Facing the bow from the stern, the left side is port and the right is starboard. The utility of such language is obvious. If told to move right, left, or back, where you move will depend on which way you happen to be facing, and it might be the wrong way. But if told to shift your weight to port, you will shift to port. If told to move aft, you will move aft. It is true, although no sailor will ever mistake fore for aft, some unthinkingly look for starboard on their right.

On an eighteenth-century sailing ship with a complexity of sail and line (Patrick O'Brien is the most readable authority), the bos'n needed to be understood when he demanded that a particular line be taut, and he did not have time to point or remonstrate. Every piece of equipment had one name and each action in relation to that object had a particular verb. Directions were then as precise as a moving ship permits. Everyone aboard knew where "west of sou'west" was. Only a helmsman, or the captain plotting a course in the chartroom, needed more exactitude than that. Words and names on such a boat attain that eighteenth-century perfection often parodied in Jonathan Swift. Swift's Laputans all carry sacks of things, all kinds of things, and point to them when they have something to say, which they likely never do.

Even on the most traditional of sailing boats today, that perfect language has deteriorated. There still may be a reason on some boats to "go below and retrieve a two-inch bell shackle," but such once-transparent words now paradoxically serve largely as salty embellishments in the language of amateur sailors. "Hard a'lee," and the seal "two points off the port bow." Will saying such things acknowledge respectfully the distance between you and Sarah Orne Jewett? Or will you sound like Roger Duncan as you speak? Or Marshall Dodge, if you are lucky, whose parodies of Maine dialect salvaged that unsettling nostalgia through its irony?

The terms now used—"sternman," "helper," "lobstering"—none of these are correct for what working on a lobster boat was in the 1960s. These delicate words were invented so that local citizens and distant television viewers who do not work in this industry could become part of it, could discuss it, could read about it in local newspapers or in books you buy at Borders, or watch on shows like *Deadliest Catch*.

In the days before commercial fishing became a socially respectable thing to do or a romantic thing to do or something one could follow on the Discovery Channel, there was no need for such words. Everyone who needed to know what the business entailed could discuss it; no one cared about the words you used for a worker or for things like baiting up or hauling back or going down the bay; or how one pointed to the rocking, the patching, the setting, or the taking up. The language of commercial fishing requires only clarity; the captain needs to communicate to the helper what needs to be done. Since what a helper is required to do is not complex, the language required to demand those actions is itself not complex, and can vary from harbor to harbor and even from boat to boat. There is no need for a conventional set of terms, since no helper is impressed from one boat to become overnight a foretopman of a nineteenth-century English frigate.

The only word I ever heard used to describe the entire scope of this work was "fishing"—lobsters were fish, and lobstering was fishing, and working on a boat that went after lobsters was working fishing. I believe the same thing is true of crabbing and scalloping and shrimping and even groundfishing. The owner of the shrimp boat in Houma, Louisiana, talked only about the glorious days we as crew might spend watching television and smoking free cigarettes in the wheelhouse. A characteristic of this language is that only those who "fish" (that is, only those who actually work on fishing boats of some kind) understand it. To everyone else, "fishing" is trawling, or dragging, or fly-fishing, or something you do for information or compliments. I still cannot say "lobstering"; there is something unnatural about it, something forced and embarrassing. Like appearing suddenly on land in one's fishing gear, or foul-weather gear, or oilskins, or simply pants, which is what the yellow, now orange, Grundéns commercial working gear used to be called. On the wharf, in such gear, you appear workmanlike, even romantic. But you cannot walk away from the boat or wharf in that gear. You would appear like Baudelaire's albatross, impeded by the magnificent wings that allow you to soar in the fishing heavens. Out of their element, these ordinary clothes change their meaning. At some point as you walk to your car or drive to town, you become, even with your Grundéns airing out on the moored boat, a thing that smells, something that needs a shave or change of clothes. You are embarrassed, stumbling on the solid land, no longer within that group of hearers who know what you mean by "fishing" and "baiting up" and why you smell the way you do. I have never seen a fisherman who did not go through this transformation.

On land with his moored boat in the background, David's accent got too thick to be natural and he appeared clumsy and ill dressed in his gray work clothes; to compensate for that, he drank, and this only made him more clumsy and uncharming and ill dressed. When David was forced to say it—it, the word "lobstering"—he stammered; when I am forced to say it, it sounds quaint and ridiculous. We went fishing. That's what we did. And when the police put us in their patrol cars for having long hair tied with a bandana and driving around at 3 AM, we waited politely, until the smell of our working clothes bore witness against our presumed malfeasance. Anything to avoid the word "lobstering," which is all the landsmen officials would understand.

In our element, we went fishing. And so it still is on the water. I would rather "get under way" or more vaguely "head out" or "go out" or say such things, and always be around those who do not require me to say the word "sailing," a word as unsettling as its grossly unprofessional counterparts in the fishing industry. Where are you going? "Sailing." It's unnatural, that word which unavoidably must appear here. I have thought I would rather make a joke of it and say "yachting." As one might say to the suspicious officer in some elaborate parody: "A-yuh." With grandfather's inflection. "On my way to go lobsterin'. A-yuh a-yuh." But someone might not hear the irony in that, and perhaps the word "sailing" doesn't sound as ridiculous to those who read it as it does to me saying it. In those days, we went fishing. We spent the summer fishing and the fishing was pretty good.

Well there.

THE WAVE

The most important thing I learned going fishing was the wave. I learned that on my first day on the boat. Before that day, there were two weeks of preparation: working on the wharf in the sun as a bad and badly and rightly badly paid carpenter, that is, a patcher of traps. With modern wire traps, there is no trap patching nor its associated ills—the briefly popular creosote dip, which neither made traps last longer nor caught more lobsters as it was rumored to do, but put many helpers, my friends among them, in the hospital recovering from creosote poisoning. So after two weeks of being a patcher of traps and $150 richer, I finally boarded the boat, on what must have been the same mid-June day that I now leave on my sailing trips. I remember briefly wondering whether I would spoil the whole thing by getting seasick. I rowed David to the moored boat and took instruction on the proper handling of oars. Fishermen do not feather their oars the way fathers diligently teach their children to do.

And on that first day aboard the boat in the light fog with the rocks to weight the traps and David's careful and precise warnings about footwork and lines running off the stern and his stories about rescuing half-drowned helpers who ignored these warnings, on that first day a family passed in an aluminum Sears boat and waved at us. Mid-June, I now realize—way too early to be out in such a boat. And at that moment time stopped for me as my heart swelled, and I thought *now now* I can ignore them, look busy, harried, professional, a working man on the water, irritated with the summer idlers in their aluminum freshwater boat. All that went through my head. I had met what some teacher, quoting Tillich, had called my *kairos*. I now understood what that pretentious term meant. I could, at age nineteen, I thought, at last play Maine for real. And as I swelled with arrogant pride, David upended these thoughts by waving back to them. He interrupted his work, this important and picturesque working on the water, this playing Maine for real—all that he interrupted without the slightest hint of irritation and he waved at the summerfolk in their aluminum boat, undersized and crank as an eggshell. "You always wave," he said, and returned to work.

You always wave, as he had waved, even when released from the mental hospital where he had been confined for putting a competitor's son headfirst into a bait barrel and nearly drowning him in the gurry. And when they cut your lines, and dragged your gear away and all the rest, and tried to drive you back to the madhouse—"The things they did!" was all he said—when they did all that, with their intricate malice, you still waved. You waved to them and to all the rest of them. And to the summerfolk, and to the kids on water skis, and he would have waved to the jet-skiers perhaps if there had been jet-skiers in those days. "You always wave," he said, resuming our important and picturesque work.

That day, this work was called "rocking."

Each trap needs ballast to sink, and wooden traps those

days had two bricks or, before the builders knew that it would dissolve in the salt, a small amount of concrete built into the base. After traps have dried out all winter long on-shore, however, that built-in two-brick ballast is not enough to sink them. You need to add ballast by rocking them, and you rock them by collecting hundreds of pounds of rocks from around the wharf and filling the lobster tank with them and adding to each trap precisely the correct size rock to make it sink. Too much, and you will have to collect and retrieve that much more rock beneath the wharf; too little, and you will have a string of what are called "floaters" behind you, which is why, in those days in the spring, you never never crossed paths with a lobster boat setting traps by going astern of it. If, in rocking these traps, you are hell-bent on risking a light trap, you need that to be the fourth or fifth trap in a string of eight. If you set that string tight enough, there might be just enough tension to pull the lightly rocked buoyant trap to the bottom. But you better warn your helper, as you throttle up and the traps fairly fly off the transom.

If all goes well, one load of rocks will be enough to weight down fifty traps, and two loads of rocks might do for all the traps you own (seven hundred, in our case), since the third fifty can be weighted with the rocks retrieved from the first fifty once they become saturated with water, and the fourth from the second. You see the same complexity in Malloy's stone-sucking procedures in Samuel Beckett's trilogy. And all these rocks must be carefully returned to the base of the pilings beneath the wharf, lest years of trap rocking remove the very foundation that keeps the wharf in place over the winter. All this once-invaluable knowledge is useless in these days of wire traps.

You always wave. And waving from the lobster boat, and from the dinghies I row, and from my own boat and others' sailboats, enviable and ridiculous, I have come to learn the subtleties of that wave hierarchy, also one worthy of Beckett, one I didn't realize then, constructing my "working man on the water wave," knowing of course that "you always wave," as others less suddenly learned than myself did not know, and expressing it in my Working Ways.

There is the raise-your-hand wave, the nerd wave, then the backward wave belt high as if the hand has been blown out, then the much advanced palm-down wave, behind one, then the palm-down, table-swabbing wave, a high parody of the standard one, and a quick elaborate parody of that wave. And as one moves up the hierarchy, one moves into the realm of commercial fishermen, and only commercial fishermen can give the high-parody palm-down wave. In a sailing boat, bearded and tanned and in Grundéns and as if framed in a camera lens, I will sometimes brave the classic palm-down wave, but usually with a wag, which makes it something more modest. If I am greeted with the High-Parodic Palm-Down Table-Swabber, I will answer with a salute or sometimes the stiff-arm, palm-out wave. But normally I try the wave-beneath-my-station wave, which is a hand high in front of the sail, arm waving wildly and obtusely nerd-like, and in a further show of deference I will make some obvious move to "go out of my way" to do all this, which is something one can do only at the higher ends of the hierarchy. A captain leaving the wheelhouse of a dragger is entitled to give however modest and ridiculous a wave he wishes and still retain his honor.

Because, as David said, you always wave. Until you learn how it can be done, you need to wave like an imbecile or absolute incompetent, because that is the truest way to felicity. A powerboat driver, hands on the wheel, will answer a wave by merely raising his hand from the wheel and glowering as if he has important things to do, which of course he does not. This places him at the bottom of the hierarchy, the nadir of watermen, as his very irritation reveals. And I believe this is what my poor father would do or would have done, not for meanness or arrogance, since he had none of that, but because he knew the science of boating was complex and too complex for any single mind even as brilliant as his own. Alas, mere complexity does not make anything important. Sailing is not an important thing to do, nor is driving a powerboat, nor, I suppose, is running a commercial lobster boat, since it is all about picturesque and unnecessary meals for tourists.

Some commercial fishermen don't make a lot of money or no one cares if they do and some are said to make so much they could buy a new truck every week. David once made a dollar a day shoveling bait, he says. I could make as much from a single string of traps back then, though one would scoff at that today. It's finally of no consequence what one makes or has made; all wave, regardless. You will see the racing sailors imagining they are worthy of respect, since maybe some work for a corporate sponsor and others merely dream of that. And real racers, I suppose, simply do not count as fishermen or cruisers, which is what this book is about. They grind away and bear and wear and stow their sails and God knows what it all means to them or to anyone else. And such racers, at the apex of self-indulgence, never never wave, because racing, like taking a powerboat out to turn a day's pay into gas, is an important thing and a too-important thing to interrupt with waves. Like, say, swimming the channel, or eating goldfish, or stealing money from investors, or stuffing what used to be a phone booth. Apart from these alien realms, you always wave.

THE BEACHMASTER

A big boat will not get you more fish, nor will a Hinckley get you any closer to whatever it is sailing is.

—Source unknown

Those who are not considered "local" (you can call them tourists or summerfolk or people who grew up in Maine but do not hold the proper political views) play Maine by imitating those considered locals. And locals play Maine by imitating those who imitate them. Even the commercial fishermen are subject to this law. The successful fisherman

plays Maine by aping those he claims to hold in contempt—
building a large shingled cottage on the water after his kids
are grown and leaving them to loaf in the ramshackle house
he raised them in. The point is made most forcefully in
James Acheson's *Lobster Gangs of Maine*. No one is happy,
it seems, with what they are, but only with the roles they
play; true happiness or success or authenticity is the happiness or success or authenticity seen in others. I don't live
in a big house because it would be too difficult to clean, too
easy to lose things in. I don't want cars and expensive floor-
ing and things that people accused of being in my class
seem to want. There is in fact nothing I want that money
could buy me. I present this as a virtue; perhaps it is a vice:
a characteristic of those summerfolk like myself who have
enough and have always had enough. What would I do, I
wonder, with that mythical Hinckley? Who would be moved
by seeing such an obviously purchased thing sail into a
fogged harbor in early June?

When hippos fight, they square off clumsily on land,
ashore, out of their native element. They spin their tails in
circles and defecate at the same time, hurling excrement all
over the beach. The winner of these matches is the Beach-
master, and I know this because I have seen it on television.
Now, according to Acheson, each harbor has a king, the
man with the biggest boat, the most investment, and the
greatest number of youthful followers. And when he gets
angry, well, in my lexicon he becomes the Beachmaster, just
like the biggest hippo in the TV show. Generally belliger-

ent, the king hippo will not cause much serious damage; hippos could not evolve if they fought to the death seeking the height of hippodom. Just so, the fisherman who actually cuts traps and assaults his rivals and sinks boats would eventually be subject to the same treatment. The Beach-master, so the theory goes, with the most gear and the largest boat, has the most to lose. So you don't need to fear when he rants about your family and mocks your educa-tion and talks about the opportunity he just missed to as-sault you. It is all intimidation, or so one thought before the recent shootings on Matinicus and elsewhere on the Mid-coast. Some say the best thing to do is simply to endure it; others say it's best to resist. But the likely consequence even of doing the right thing is only a degree more or less of ver-bal abuse.

The only certain danger comes not from the Beach-master but from his minions, the little hippos, who seek to ingratiate themselves with the master. It is those who might cut a mooring line, hoping that "would teach you." This is something no Beachmaster would condone. Boats do not and must not go ashore, and no one responsible enough to own a large working boat wants to see that happen. Like my own idiot students who think they imitate me by being con-trary or loud, the baby hippos will one day grow out of it.

The greater and the lesser hippos alike are excellent bor-rowers. I had, long ago, balloon-like rubber rollers once used, I think, to stabilize freight in railway cars. You could launch a three-hundred-pound skiff on two of these with ease, rolling it down a bank and up that same bank for the winter. When these rollers were discovered by a local herring fisherman, he asked to borrow them. For his dories, so he said. I use them, I said. "I'll bring them back." They are deflated, I said. "I'll patch them." I never saw them again. Every year, pushing the skiff over makeshift wooden rollers becomes more difficult for me. Another garrulous charmer borrowed an old hunting rifle of mine, and sold it, obviating its return. This same man taught fishing to an in-law, who as a consequence of this tutelage loaded his own .308, which had once brought down the largest deer I have ever seen, and put a round through the outboard of what he claimed was a low-life competitor. A neighbor too plays Maine by playing at commercial fishing. He has relieved me of excess material for years: parts of old trailers, line, still functional, even an old skiff. He too "will patch them," so he says, but I never see them again, except rotting on his shore. Gear goes missing. But gear, as not all things, is easily replaceable.

It's best to treat such creatures with respect, but not with undue sentiment; it's best to leave them spinning their tails and excrement, and that is what I believe is best to do here.

NAMEBOARDS

All my boats have come to me with names, since I never bought one new or had one built for me. Even more than the words "lobstering" or "sailing," which I use here only for communication's sake, there is something unutterable to me about these names. You can find the name for David's boat in this book, but if you want to know the name for my boat, you will have to look for it in a photo or deduce it from a reference to other boats. I see it on the registration papers, on the stern. I hear my friends ask me how "she" (my boat, naming it) is, as if this were the salty or nautical or Down East thing to do, and I always hesitate, then say, "Fine. The boat is fine." And I have never referred to my boat, however loved, as "she" or as a feminine thing, or by its name, or incorrectly as a "ship," as some sailors incredibly do.

The name that came with this boat, I thought, was clearly a product of that hideous decade, the 1970s. The name of a raptor, or weapon, or some violent thing, with some small change, in this case an otiose final *e*, as if this reference were a pure accident. You can see such names in the movies and TV shows from that loathsome period: *Remington Steele, Bullitt, Magnum, P.I.*, and, yes, before that, things were likely no different, since there were shows like *Peter Gunn* in my childhood, and even *Bullitt* is from 1968. The nameboard had been removed, and the name itself, the owner claimed, "reserved" for the boat that had replaced it. As it happened, he hadn't really reserved that name at all, not in its pure form, since years later, he passed me, bound east just off Fuller Rock where I was sailing, now west, with Linda Jane. We stared at each other through the binoculars, since Charlie and Nancy's boat was a Cape Dory 33 like his, and mine, seen in the distance, was "like," he must have thought, the old boat he had sold to me. When I saw the name *Hawke II* on the stern, we both began waving wildly, and I excitedly told Linda Jane: "That's him. Look! the guy who sold me the boat. And look at him wave at us! He's saying 'Look! Look! There he is. That's the kid I sold the boat to.'" "No he's not," she said as she stroked away the lines on my face.

There was, I knew, no legal basis for such "reserve of names," and the ethics were subject, not to our handshake, but to two competing schools of thought on boat names, both zealously defended. The first sees names as permanent, like the names you give your children: you cannot change the name of a boat once it is christened, any more than you could launch it bow-first or paint it blue (or was it green?), as the sea always "claims its own." The second sees names as arbitrary whims of the owner, and when the boat changes hands, these can change as well. During the eighteenth and early nineteenth centuries, when sailors fought and killed each other and stole each others' ships (true ones, that is), this was routine, and captured ships with gay French names were immediately Anglicized when refitted. Each of these schools has variant traditions: "Laura," for example, of the *Laura B.* out of Port Clyde, likely refers to the wife or daughter of the man who ordered the boat, and the initial *B.* obliquely to the name of the builder. You will find all these schools and opinions represented by the boats of my home port in, say, the *Tryphena*

Chandler, the *Stuart Little,* and the series of *Mary Mary*s, whose skilled owner I first met as he casually backed one of them under sail into the makeshift slips of the marina.

I believed myself a member of the first school of thought, and I must have gotten this from David, since Father routinely named whatever boat he had, whatever its origin. Thus, there was nothing I could do about this name with its otiose final *e*. I considered various options: I could, I thought, put the name in small letters. I could also, I imagined, place a large and prominent *II* on the stern, letting it stand for the real name without announcing it. I could, I thought, do all these things, but all were matters of thumbing my nose at tradition, and if I felt that way about these traditions and superstitions, I might just as well rename the boat *Linda Jane* and be done with it. And all the while, with its blank stern, the boat never quite sailed as well for me as the old boat it replaced.

Finally, having had enough of this nonsense of names, I simply gave in: I had nothing to do with my own name, and if there are those who don't like it (my Midwest friends cannot bring themselves to use the two syllable full form I introduce myself with), then that is their problem, not mine. And if I have difficulty with my boat's name, that is my problem and needs to be fixed. I called the sign painter, and he put the boat's name on the stern with the largest capitals in his repertory. That fall, I discovered that the name had no otiose final *e* at all and had nothing to do with the bad action movies of the '70s. Instead, it was the name of a famous (but not to me) English admiral of what I'll call the "classic age of sail." I read no more of that admiral, and the boat has sailed in perfect tune with me ever since.

I left fishing and went sailing because with Father gone and David in a state of decay and Linda Jane on the continent somewhere it seemed right to do such things. Such boating, I thought, would be truly mine and never theirs. Yet as the years pass, those who know any pair of us think otherwise. They think that way because, I imagine, they do not have the sequence of years right: Father and my fishing on the water and Linda Jane; they misimagine or misrepresent these histories that never coincided or in any way intersected, except, perhaps, in a phone call or two ("Don't you think," David said, having called earlier from the east side of Harpswell and left a message with my father, "that Nate's accent has suddenly gotten awfully thick?"). Or perhaps it was Father in the water and my hard working hands on my hips, watching him guide the dinghy to shore that day whose precise history I can never seem to get quite right. Or perhaps it is the Bank Lobby Episode, where I rant on some inconsequential point of procedure or ethics and perform in front of the bank tellers in what I consider a perfect expression of my own singularity. One of the tellers laughs: "It's so wonderful to hear you like this; why, we so miss the way your father used to come in here and . . ." Each catastrophe seemed once so singular—love, the death and loss of loved ones and relations. We are unique, we think, in these, despite the billions of dead parents and young and delusional lovers like ourselves.

I walk in the snow in South Dakota. Years later, I will be walking through a different snow with Linda Jane, talking of her dead husband. I see an owl rise from the corner of the flat-roofed building of the landlocked university. I marvel at the white burst caught in the streetlights. I think of this owl as a mere entity—no one, I think, has yet found meaning in such things. I forget, surprisingly, the trite symbolism from the classical tradition and the medieval tradition I am supposed to know. The owl is of course a foreboding of death. It will be a week before I make the connection.

I feel at home in the new-fallen snow, although I no longer experience new-fallen snow, except in sickness or in tragedy. I came to the Maine snow the winter John died. And I came to the Maine snow after Linda Jane's surgery. I came to Maine to comfort her, and instead spent a week playing Maine in the woods with her stupidly enthusiastic dog. And it reminds me of the less expected snow hitting my face on that last sailing day with her, before she realized I would really not be coming back to her.

It is June again, and Linda Jane walks away from me on the dry trail in the San Gabriels, walks away from me on the airport concourses; Father, wasted from chemotherapy, staggers across the college quad; David lifts his head in astonishment from the hospital bed.

PART III
MIDCOAST

CHAPTER SEVEN

THE KENNEBEC

Just don't touch the bulb while you're standing in the bathtub.

—Miss Dove, landlady in Topeka,
reported by Linda Jane

Sailing and yachting magazines are full of too-crafted narratives called tales, or yarns as they were once known. They contain clauses of mock self-deprecation such as "we should have taken down the spinnaker in the thirty-knot breeze" or understatement, like the very phrase "thirty-knot breeze." They take place in exotic locales: "on our way to Bermuda . . ." "while cruising past Baja . . ." I suppose the magazines commission them from professionals, and edit the inaccuracies of the sailing terminology away with other professionals. Perhaps their readers concoct them and send them in, and the professionals edit the inaccuracies of their recollections away. The authors, or the editors' version of their authors, are confident and unruffled; they are competent and strong, strangely English, like Adlard Coles of *Heavy Weather Sailing*, on which these narratives are often modeled. Like Coles himself, whose 1967 voice has largely disappeared in what is called the "fifth revised edition of 1999," these narrators are subject to misfortune, which they endure, like Coles, with intense interest and a sanguine spirit. The incidents they describe form no larger narrative; as singulars, each is another satisfying and untaxing episode of *Law and Order* or *CSI* or, for those of us growing up in the 1950s, *Perry Mason*. I claim to be done reading such stories and done with the glossy advertisements for the expensive glossy gear that surrounds these stories. Adventures that are worth relating are today the consequence of incompetence or stupid mistakes.

And that brings me to Linda Jane and the offshore storm (or what I described as one). It brings me back to my first boat and the send-off of Bump Orr, who sold insurance and chased bluefin tuna and once convinced the IRS these costs were deductible (so he says) with his protest, "I can't help being a bad fisherman." "May the wind be at your back," he said, thinking prayers, like insurance sales themselves, were charms. He did not calculate, experienced boater though he was, that for a trip from Belfast to Harpswell, that is, from the northeast to the southwest, a wind at your back would mean three days of northeast winds and swells that grew so high they buried the hull of the boat sailing next to you in the trough of the waves. He did not consider that after the second day there would be no boats at all, seen or unseen in the troughs, just you, with no experience of sailing, and Linda Jane sitting at the helm looking complacent and brave and whose bravery was the only thing that kept you from crying out and giving up the whole stupid notion of sailing. But rock-hard Linda Jane with her white captain's hat, imitating Father's inappropriate captain's cap, pulled down over her fair skin and red hair, had never sailed. She simply assumed this was the way things always were, more or less as they were in the more harrowing of sailing movies. Just as Linda Jane, some two decades later, on her first sail, would watch me put two reefs in the main and hank on the working jib, and sail luffingly around the harbor for a cautious hour in deference to her. And calmly she would merely think that this is how it is; not bad, she thought, steady and fearless sailor that she instantly became.

A boat of the size of my first boat should not have been making that trip, especially when skippered by one who hoped he was competent because he once worked on commercial fishing boats, but who didn't know the weather or what the waves might mean or what the phrase "ugly chop" in the *United States Coast Pilot* might refer to when used of the opposition of wind and tide inside Seguin, in the mouth of the Kennebec. That is really most of the story, apart from the details of small boats surfing on waves generated by the opposition of wind and tide in the mouth of the Kennebec. You can find plenty of these narratives, with far more graphic detail, in the glossy sailing magazines. I remember only the face of the following wave, which Coles and one of the recent editions of Bowditch's *American Practical Navigator* claim was likely one-half the height of what a competent sailor would estimate. I thus can't say what a wave I saw then as "high as the spreader" might actually have been.

It is the ancillary story that concerns me here, the story about the father of Linda Jane. Dan was wonderfully calm and ironic and serene, and he smiled gracious half-smiles as he struggled to accept the man next to his daughter as what that man obviously was. He was an Episcopal priest, I think, or maybe he taught at a major university. In any case, he knew and had experienced most of the intricacies of the human mind and all its frailties. He could consequently afford his irony in ways many of us could not, we who used our trenchant ironies to cover our mere fears and ignorance. Thus the diffidence of our language of the water; thus the litotes so common in the sailing magazines.

Dan was a sailor, so Linda Jane said, and had once owned a small open boat. From somewhere in New Jersey he drove to the marina on the Hudson River every weekend, where he sailed his nineteen-foot open boat in the grandness of the waterway. The boat must have been a Rhodes, and the Rhodes 19 keeps appearing in my life. Linda Jane herself owned a Rhodes, decades later; and she named it *Circe,* since it turned all men who boarded it into swine. And my neighbor Philip has one too, which I helped him launch a few days ago; there is a fleet of them in Cundys Harbor from which Chuck took the pattern for *Circe*'s rudder, and Linda Jane's father sailed such a Rhodes 19 in the Hudson on the weekend. Flying from Newark to

Maine for the summer, I always note the small marinas tucked deeply into the banks of the river.

When I lost Linda Jane for the last time, we were sailing such a boat when the rudder that had been rotting for years sheered off at the waterline, and we sailed it back to the mooring on the jib and an oar. The genius Chuck redesigned and built the rudder from scratch in a day, although his hands were all gone from arthritis and carpal tunnel and my relation to Linda Jane was all gone from frustration and the boat itself was all gone from years of patchwork repairs. That boat once sailed swift as she sang tuneless in the Penobscot sun. And then I was gone and the boat too finally gone into other hands. And Linda Jane waits for my return on the sun-filled porch.

Dan's story, whether told by me or by Linda Jane herself, involves sailing and storms and loss, like so many others. But as I tell his story, you will see it as strangely devious. Linda Jane told it as a straightforward sailing tale, and she wasn't really familiar with tales of this kind. Every weekend in the summer, in the story told by Linda Jane, Dan drove to the Hudson and sailed the boat he loved, that Rhodes 19, as I now identify it, a boat that keeps appearing in my memory. Linda Jane told me about this love earnestly, as if to prove to me she understood the power and the magic and the love of the water. This, it is said, was the very emotion that had gripped even her dad, who knew enough of life to be, I suppose, indifferent to all but its most inexorable of drives.

The Rhodes 19 remained moored or docked in the Hudson one fall perhaps longer than it should have, or so she said; perhaps it should have been hauled and stored in September like most of the boats even in Maine are hauled and stored, but she would have no way of knowing that. And so, in her tale, late on the river, when the inevitable storm came, the boat was lost. It didn't sink; it was not wrecked. It broke free of its moorings, or what there were of moorings on the river, or worked its insidious way from the tiny finger piers visible from a passing aircraft and "was lost." That was the magic and the pain of it.

The father of Linda Jane then continued each weekend to drive to the Hudson in search of the lost hull. He could not give that boat up, the Rhodes 19 that keeps appearing here in its characteristic shape, rudder off the stern, the mast raked aft. He drove and searched longingly from the roadways. And once, Linda Jane said, he claimed to have caught, he thought, a glimpse of it, by the bridge, he said, and that was enough, she guessed, and soon the weekend trips to the Hudson in search of the wrecked or unwrecked or drifting or renamed lost hull were over and Dan resumed his ironic stares surrounded by his flock or perhaps his bored and ambitious students at the university.

And that, as anyone can see, except Linda Jane, who could not see, as stoically she steered through what I may as well call "mountainous ocean swells from the offshore storm"—that is not a story about sailing or storms or wrecked hulls, or the love of the water and the air, or the serendipity of one's course in the wind and currents. You might spend time looking for a lost child or a lost love or a lost moment of your past, but boats, finally, are machines and replaceable, even though the emotions involved in them might not be. However precise Dan's tale was, told by Linda Jane, however moving its depictions of emotions, so revealing of the love of man for the water and the boats, it was the product of a professional, and you cannot trust a professional for details. It is, finally, like all sailing stories.

The story is, rather, about rendezvous, and illicit love, and the most ordinary of affairs, and pain, and loss, and lying to one's loved ones, and long trips to the Hudson in search of love, or argument, or at least a final resolution. For it was certainly not a boat or a wrecked hull or a Rhodes 19 or whatever it was or parted moorings or neglect of a marina that took Dan to the Hudson on the weekend; and it was not a swamped hull that he was able to salvage one last glimpse of that day on the unnamed bridge of the story.

Thinking of this story now, of those bad seas with Linda Jane, I think of other days. And if all days were like the placid days on the water, I think, everyone would be a sailor. There are days when all is so easy and the breeze so cool and consistent on one's face and the entire sea so unthreatening that perhaps this is what sailing is or can be; yes, everyone would be a sailor under such conditions. The ground will be fertile and weed-free and you can be a farmer or an astronaut or a schoolteacher leading attentive students from the darkness or work in the woods or live off the groceries you sell to your neighbors. You will forget then about the days when the rain has soaked all the spare gear, days when the contrived romance of it all fails and you wonder only what it is like to be warm and dry with the worry of mere bills and gas prices and sports events. Everyone will believe your stories then, being young with Linda Jane, while the lost imagined hull drifts in the circulating currents of the river.

WHALE SIGHTING

Linda Jane is twenty. And I will never feel what I felt then. It is, I think, the first full season of my first boat, the first year after the mountain-high seas and the duplicitous stories of the search for the lost hull on the Hudson. Sailing was all pretense then. So un-Coles-like, I was nervous of the water, the way the boat heeled in the facing wind and yawed away from it, its very grace through the water. Like my father, I longed for the perfect days and resented the imperfect days and my resentment made such imperfect days worse.

Linda Jane is young. And I will never, I think, feel this way again. It was one of my first trips up the coast by boat, where even the short, well-marked courses to the Sheepscot and to MacMahan Island and past the Cuckolds to Boothbay Harbor seemed adventurous.

I loved Linda Jane with what I was certain was my last passion, and I experienced with her my last true jealousy. I had thought, over a dozen years earlier, so much earlier it seemed to me then that I had, in some Nietzschean way, overcome that emotion. Linda Jane had left me. She would be gone, she said, for a week, I believe. She was visiting another lover. To tell him goodbye, she said. It was 1971. We were hippies, we claimed. It is what promiscuous hippies did. Nonetheless, all this is still difficult to speak of. Thinking of those days, I become, still, hesitant and defensive. And the weeks were far longer in those days than weeks are today.

I sit in the living room of the cheap apartment in Bath, Maine, in 1971. There is no question of sleep. I play records I have since lost and repurchased and a select few are still there in my obsolete record collection. I sit cross-legged in the living room as beautiful as twenty-four-year-olds are beautiful and as the young Linda Jane was beautiful. I had been fishing that summer. I could not be stronger; I could not have been more fit. The sores on my arms from the bait were gone; the sunburn had tanned. I walked tall again, and without the hunched-over, round-shouldered gait of those who spend their working lives on the water. And I thought without anger that I simply wanted that other lover dead. The emotion was simple and rational, the thought clear and unqualified. I wanted him dead in a way that I have never wanted other rivals dead—those rivals of earlier juvenile love you just wish humiliated in some mysterious way that will in some even more mysterious and undefined way lead to your vindication. I did not that night care about vindication. I wanted a universe free of that lover, and I had never felt such callous and focused jealousy. I vowed then, sitting with the records strewn around me, Tom Rush, I think, and Delaney and Bonnie and Friends, I think it was, never to indulge myself in these lesser jealousies again, since any petty jealousy I might feel in the future and had felt in the past would desecrate this moment.

Linda Jane is twenty and these are feelings I say I will never have again.

There was nothing about her that I did not desire. It could be her face, a face so angelic my mother's friend likened her to a medieval miniature. It could have been the perfectly athletic body, or the agelessness of her features, which still today retain in a fifty-year-old the image of those days. And I loved her introversion and the brooding that eventually forced me from her life and left me lying on the spot where we first sat on the lawn behind my house, lying there and sobbing and pounding the grass with my fist.

For Linda Jane was never mine, of course. She was never mine, and it was not just that moment we took the bus to Boston and she told me, more bravely than one would expect from one so young, that her feelings were no longer there. And I became that ridiculous schoolchild again—how could it be that my own emotions did not matter? Why aren't my feelings, alone, sufficient?

I have done many evil and petty things to her: I have lied to her, I have tricked her, pretended to support her, followed her, read her mail, and determined things about her that we have never breathed a word of. I have loved her and felt her push me away and elicited promises only made so she could sleep; and I have experienced again and again her leaving me, without a word, without a note, to reappear in some distant city—Boston, or Topeka, or Seattle, or Moscow, for God's sake. And thirty years later, she is still in my life, and when we sail, there is still her distant stare and her indifference to the water. Just her stare across the water that she must have inherited from the father we both so love.

The Sheepscot River is just past the Kennebec on the coast, and opens to a large bay where the tides run too quickly and the chop, as Bill Sr. recently described it to me, "just stacks up." In Ebenecook Harbor, it is said the old schooners waited out a foul tide, but the tides are nearly always foul just west of the Sheepscot, where the spill from the Kennebec flows determinedly east to west, despite the tide. You can go upriver. You can take the inside passage through the Townsend Gut to Boothbay, but that entails using the engine. That entails, too, memories of sailing into Boothbay in fog and too many visions of Linda Jane, young and old, sailing in from Pemaquid or east around the Cuckolds.

My Linda Jane lies bored in that small first boat becalmed in the east-to-west wash in the mouth of the Kennebec. Ahead, a humpback whale arches toward us through the water on a perfect reciprocal course, or so it seems, mark to mark. I shout to the boat behind me, "Did you see the whale?" "No." Then, halving the speaking distance between us, the whale breaches, spout, back, and finally we will see the majestic tail. And Linda Jane awakened has her camera. In the image, the man in the following boat is on the bow, eyes widened doubtless, the back of the whale is aligned with him, and this is moments before I say, now in a normal tone of voice, "Did you see him that time?"

Yet in the picture, taken with a 50mm lens, that is not the story you see, and you of course hear nothing. You do not see the thirty yards between us, nor hear us speaking in little more than normal voices. You do not see the shockingly minimal distance, and you do not see me, and you do not see the lovely and athletic Linda Jane, whose unselected lens is responsible for the illusion of distance that appears there. As you gaze at the photo, in an increasingly unfamiliar black-and-white, you will hear only my retelling of the story, redescribing the fabulous breaching of the whale, retelling of my love for Linda Jane, and recalling the trip to the Sheepscot and to Boothbay, when she lay in the sun and burned a pattern into her back still visible years afterwards. I assume the whale is now dead, or merged completely into the others I have seen, or lost in the stories I have told about them. And Linda Jane still keeps the distance she projected into the photo with the wide-angle lens.

WEDDING ALBUM

In the contrary currents running past the ledges at Seguin Island, I know that Linda Jane got married today. In the future, one will say it was a simple ceremony with family and friends. But there is nothing simple about this ceremony, I think, addressed as it is solely to the doting families. The

rest of us, who have known Linda Jane for years, listen un-
comfortably as the words grow more and more predictable
and her former husband, so loved by us, recedes more and
more into the oblivion he has avoided since his death three
years ago. I imagine his face, and others there imagine his
face as well. They say he is laughing and deriding these for-
malities. But I am not sure this is the case. He was shy, and
inarticulate. There were no ironies about him, even dead,
and there was nothing he could be imagined to express on
this day.

Linda Jane got married today.

You would think Linda Jane would just brazen the
whole thing out somewhere in the plains of Nebraska and
not bring this back to California. Or that the hippie husband, fixing his Volkswagon buses down there near Boston
in the late 1960s, would just drink his beer and speak as he
was told to speak. You would think the folderol of fidelity
would begin to appear just forced: those visions of new adventures, and futures, and lifelong commitments. That the
new breeze you felt would be just another sailing breeze,
not one to cancel all other sailing days.

Linda Jane got married today.

Linda Jane got married today and I played my hippie
music all the way home, from the resort with the mani-
cured lawns and the cheap food and through the road construction and past all the back-to-earthers' farmland and
over the dirt roads and finally down the newly paved road
to Harpswell. It is a drive I am repeating from forty years

ago, when I lost the image of the Georgetown ceremony in the roar of the motorcycle, and a future such as this one seemed unimaginable.

There was a wedding photo of Linda Jane in the papers years ago, or perhaps it was no wedding photo, but some grotesque parody of the famous photo of Verdi, arms all akimbo, and his librettist Boito. She is in California with her new consort, who has grown fat and complacent with Linda Jane beside him. "Garroted by Sparafucile, she still sang," I will later write of this Italianate fiasco.

With that churchful of poseurs in Georgetown on the Sheepscot, I watched in distress as Linda Jane walked down the aisle with her hippie husband and her ridiculous white dress. She claims later she recognized that distress and wanted to pause to assure me this bourgeois pomp wouldn't last; it was all just parody and ultimately made no difference. Yet she did not break her pace in that church aisle to salve that juvenile despair, just as Linda Jane some decades later did not so much as glance at us, and just as Linda Jane would leave Nebraska with her consort without a word to me. She is beautiful for her age, as she always was beautiful, but life has made its inevitable mark on her, as she negotiates the rough passages near her beloved Seguin Island in the mouth of the Kennebec. In New York with her, her hippie husband gone at last, I lie with her in the roar of the Deegan Expressway. Her arm is around me; she turns suddenly away. I drive in the silence to New Orleans.

CHAPTER EIGHT

BOOTHBAY HARBOR

I do not know which to prefer:
The beauty of inflections
Or the beauty of innuendoes.
The blackbird whistling
Or just after.

—Wallace Stevens

The next harbor or series of harbors east of the Sheepscot is Boothbay Harbor, and the two sets of harbors are held apart by a rock and lighthouse absurdly named the Cuckolds. Entering or leaving this harbor is easier than entering or leaving any other Maine harbor, but because of that, its history is one of obstructions: Linda Jane unhappy with the position of the boat as it drifts too closely to the moored boats; the challenge from the residents of Squirrel Island, who claim rights to the surrounding water; and, what concerns me here, the fog. Although the fog in Maine is said to be worse the farther one works east, the densest fogs are not those recorded in weather reports and synopses, not those found in the archives and histories, but rather the fogs that are experienced. If I ever learned to navigate in fog, it was in the unchallenging waters of Boothbay.

Despite the dicta of tradition, it is never too cold or too hot or wet or sunny or rainy or windblown for fog. It is never the wrong location or the wrong season; nor is it ever the wrong time of day. There is fog for each season in Maine, and there are fogs for each section of the Maine coast. There is, for example, the fog I have today, the day I am writing or revising, as the sun is casting dark shadows and I can see even to the closest shore. I am on my boat writing or revising this, or perhaps I am at home, looking out over a narrow bay as the fog pushes into the Basin at Harpswell. There is also the fog of yesterday, where the land was uniformly gray. And in the books, you will see described the difference between convection fog and the offshore fog brought in by a southeast breeze, and warm fogs, and cold fogs. These technical variants I experience the same way, since while sailing, all that matters is fog density and wind.

There are fogs that, even for an amateur like me, are worth sailing in, worth the calculation of one's course, and there are fogs that sailors like me should prudently endure at anchor. There are fogs that clear and others that hide thunderstorms and depressing ones that last for days, and fogs that in the right light create marvels out of Down East islands left by the enfolding depths of the earth and the recession of glaciers. There are fogs that permit an hour or two of sailing or motoring late in the day, and give you the experience of resting all day and getting in a sail as well. Then the fogs so close you don't have to sail at all, or the ones that form during the evening or surprise you at mid-day, or the ones the dude schooners sail in and out of, with the tourists taking turns blowing their tiny foghorns, or the ones that define a sailing trip from the beginning. There are the vagaries of light that connect one year to another, or two places to each other, suddenly identical in the mist. Or, more dangerously, a string of navigational buoys with their numbers appallingly disordered and confused.

The worst fogs I've experienced on the Midcoast were those when I worked for David. I knew then nothing of the water, and worked in the stern of the boat, doing what I was told to do, tying knots and baiting irons and moving traps starboard to port and measuring fish and emptying the bait box as I was told to do. There is really nothing to this kind of work if you are intelligent enough to do what you are told to do by someone you know knows better. But it is not an easy thing to do as you are told to do.

David brought one of his kids aboard each weekend. It might be young David or Colie or one of the others, and for the most part, until they were old enough to work for real, they would just bait irons for me. At thirteen, Colie, a tougher man than I would grow to be, considered me a god, but it was only, he admits, because I could blow smoke rings in the late-morning breeze. Toward the end of the day, David would theatrically give up the wheel to the chosen child, and the boat course, headed in, would become erratic. For six days, alone with me, David had uttered nothing but the most precise directives, and now he would panic, it seems, shouting out to them suddenly ambiguous and unintelligible orders. Even Colie would consequently screw up the lines or screw up at the wheel as I would never err in the stern, and David would then curse and blame them for all the evils on the water. There really is nothing to this work if you are smart enough to do what you are told to do. But you must be told clearly what it is you are to do.

That first summer was historic, I am told, for fog, but for me, the three clear days we experienced in July were simply days like all the other days. I am certain I have told myself this anecdote before. I am certain I have said, "I one day stood on the stern of the thirty-six-foot wooden lobster boat; I wanted to see if there would be a day I could say, 'the fog was so thick, I could not see the bow from the stern.'" I remember this clearly and I remember I could in fact say what I intended to say—that the fog was so dense, I could not see *Tarn's* bow from the stern. But I cannot, in good faith, remember what it was I saw on that morning. The universe of the helper on a lobster boat is only the open area of the stern behind the wheelhouse. And whatever the conditions, I don't see how the bow would be visible from such a position. On a lobster boat, the wheelhouse stands amidships, and from the stern, that wheelhouse, with its instruments, and twin vertical exhaust, and David leaning forward toward the glass, is all anyone would see. How could the bow seem framed in the fogged glass windows of the wheelhouse? Did I imagine that? And how could I remember such a strange and unnatural sight? both the bow invisible through the wheelhouse glass, and the bow as it might be imagined there? To see forward, the helper leans over the rail, supported by his muscled arms. Or perhaps, proclaiming a moment of indolence, he sits in high non-chalance smoking and blowing smoke rings on the wash rail.

The only instruments we had aboard were a depth sounder and a compass I am told was never used, even in the fog such as we experienced that first July. The depth sounder was a circular panel with a blip marking the depths, and although David watched it scrupulously, to me those blips seemed arbitrary, and I suspected, knowing nothing, that he did not really check the depths but merely pretended to, just as I, in life, so often go through the motions of, say, checking the depth or the weather, or a scholarly reference, and take credit for that, rather than procuring for myself any real information. The blips on the Raytheon were orange in the fog. There was one that indicated the depth and another (or was it more?) called an echo, which you had to disregard. To me there were simply two or three blips on the screen, and intently as David stared at them, I saw no difference at the precise moment he released the first trap of the string into the water. There was never a sudden movement in the reading on the Raytheon to tell him, "Here! The underwater valley where the fish molt. *Here.*" And I wonder if in those days it mattered much where the traps settled on the bottom, even though David derided the workers in the skiffs who "didn't know where the holes were." I wondered if it mattered much in those days, before the electronic gear and the navigational instruments destroyed the fishing industry that for generations had lived on its own inefficiencies.

There were three clear days in July that year. I have told myself for years that there were three clear days in July, that there were days so thick you could not see the bow from the stern. But I cannot, in good faith, distinguish that year on the water from the subsequent years on the water in the same working boat.

The Raytheon swings through the valleys on the ocean floor.

THE HARBORMASTER

There was an evening fog one night as I stayed in Lewis Cove in Linekin Bay, the only place you can anchor safely and legally in the Boothbay region. I had sailed to Boothbay years earlier in my small boat and anchored badly in the harbor, much to Linda Jane's annoyance, first in the area cleared for the touring boats, and second over in the wash of Capitol Island, where an owner of a cabin on the shore motored by in his Boston Whaler and we were young enough that he told us to take the free mooring next to us. That time, I remember, I was with Linda Jane, the beautiful daughter of a local fisherman, and then married, incestuously it seemed, to my brother-in-law. She had set her eyes on educated inland men to take her away from this life of no hot water and baths in the tub in the kitchen and the smell of bait and the brutal charm of fishermen. And she secured those educated men with ease, until one of them, my brother-in-law, became enamored of the life she wanted to escape, and married her for it, and they lived for years in the smell of bait and the charming tales of the fishermen, and all he ever did was rig the place for hot water. When he became uselessly addicted to cocaine and to his version of life on the water, she took her appalling beauty away and escaped to inland horses and farmland. I wondered, staring at her . . . I wondered . . .

I am listening to Camden Marine Radio in Boothbay, now years later in the fog, when Channel 16 overrides the soporifics of these overheard conversations with a call of measured distress. I will struggle again to avoid the language of sailing manuals in this story, but it will be difficult, since the key characters were enmeshed in that language.

Boothbay can be thought of as a series of bays, Boothbay Harbor proper on the west, Linekin Bay to the east. Farther to the east is a third bay, actually a river, the Damariscotta River. And beyond that is Johns Bay, which leads to the Pemaquid of Linda Jane but is of no consequence in this story. It is amusing to me that despite the number of times I have sailed through this area, I need a chart to describe even the simplest and most basic of its features. There is a wide peninsula between Linekin Bay, where I was anchored, and the Damariscotta River. On the west shore of the Damariscotta River, cutting into the wide peninsula separating it from Linekin Bay, there is a small river called Little River. This small river is navigable for a very short distance and ends finally in a cul-de-sac no more than a few hundred yards into the land.

For this tale, all you need to know, I think, are three locations. Boothbay Harbor in the west bay (the homeport of the harbormaster), Linekin Bay in the middle, which will form no part of the narrative, the wide and navigable Damariscotta River beyond that, and the peninsula cut by the Little River between the two.

But even as I describe this, I realize that the details are recalcitrant, and I need to revise my description to make this at all intelligible. So I will modify the setting and describe merely the two bays: Boothbay Harbor, the Damariscotta, and the peninsula and Little River between them. Linekin Bay is irrelevant to the story, except insofar as I am anchored in Linekin Bay, listening to the VHF radio. You can imagine how much more difficult envisioning all this would be in fog.

The call came in the evening from two fishermen, that is to say, not commercial fishermen but casual fishermen like you and me, in an open boat with lines and fishing rods and cases of beer and a bad outboard to boot. They were caught in the fog in the Damariscotta River, and it was now dark, and affordable GPS would be years in the future. It would be easier in the tale below to say they were in Linekin Bay itself, but this would also entail moving the geographical location of the Little River. The old harbormaster answered gruffly from Boothbay Harbor. On a foggy night on a boat, everyone listened then to VHF and perhaps still does when there is no other form of entertainment. And knowing he was being so monitored by all the boats anchored in the bay on that foggy evening, the harbormaster declared in his best Maine accent that he would come and get them and radar and GPS and Loran, none of which he carried, be damned. He would rescue them the old way, just as, say, they had done in the old days before radio and distress calls. The same old days, maybe, when they generated electricity with windmills.

I listened to Channel 68, I believe it was, and followed the harbormaster as he made his angry and expert way deftly around the first peninsula and past Spruce Point, separating Boothbay Harbor and Linekin Bay, and then made the straight and open run to Linekin Neck, separating the complex of bays in Boothbay from the Damariscotta River, and maybe getting as confused in the fog and the night as I am in the telling it and saying, "Just wait, I'm coming . . . Just flash your light overhead."

I don't remember whether I heard his engine, but I must have in the calm night and the fog. And then he came over the radio again and saw the light of the distressed fishermen, or claimed to, and feeling his way around Linekin Neck in the fog, expecting it to open up into the Damariscotta River, where those fishermen were desperately awaiting him, he headed smartly for that light and then something went awry which he did not detail or describe at all over Channel 68 on the VHF and his boat . . . Was it nearly ashore? And where ashore?

He then brought out his official blue light, or so he said, which I imagine only the harbormaster is authorized to carry, and flashed it, so he claimed, overhead. I, less than a mile away in the fog, saw nothing, although I must have thought to look for it. "Do you see my blue light?" he asked with contrived and obvious irritation at the stupid summerfolk who had stayed too long fishing in the fog in the Damariscotta River in an open boat. "Uh . . ." but the river-bound fishermen could not of course acknowledge this in the proper way and were subject to more of the harbormaster's radio-transmitted scorn. He then expertly steered his official harbormaster boat toward the light of the stranded fishermen until it would steer no more, having run into rocks, it seemed, "These rocks!" he snarled, and each time thwarted by them in the dark and the fog, he would turn on his blue light and spit at those he was rescuing, "Do you see my blue light?" and in great irritation would demand again whether they could see it, which of course they could despite "These damn rocks!" And finally they asked, with all the obsequious respect they could: "Should we call for help?" "Well, I thought" he said, rock-bound and contemptuous, "that was what I was doing."

The harbormaster, of course, had competently navigated to Linekin Neck in the fog and in the dark. All he had to do then was to give that peninsula a "wide berth" and swing north into the mouth of the Damariscotta River and steam straight to the grateful and helpless fishermen. Instead, he had timorously followed the shoreline, and instead of entering the wide sweep of the bay, minutes from making his dramatic rescue of the stupid summerfolk, he had crept carefully along the bank and consequently run right up the Little River—the narrow channel that cuts into the peninsula he should have passed completely. And the devious river trickled straight north toward the hapless fishermen and their flashing light, then, after a hundred yards or so, dwindled completely into the rocks and banks and fields that marked the east bank of the river. And past "These Rocks!" and fields, impassable by boat, of course, the stranded fishermen flashed their lights. Stuck in the middle of Linekin Neck with no outlet before him, and with no crew to blame for his mistakes, the rock- and river-bound harbormaster berated those he was attempting to save.

This story has no victims. Remarkably few boaters are killed or injured in such incidents. But it has at least one kind character, a commercial fisherman anchored nearby in an offshore dragger equipped with radar, then the preferred navigational equipment, and he, as I, had been amusing himself by listening indolently to the VHF, and he, as I, had realized what Bill the harbormaster had done, but instead of saying, "Hey, Bill, you're in the Little River, you damn idiot; back your ass south out of there and . . ." he said, "Hey, Bill. I got my radar here; I'm just anchored in the bay. I'll go and get them." Which he did, without, I recall, a single word on the VHF.

I never found out how Bill found his way out of the Little River or whether he ever realized he had been there at all, or whether he continued to serve his doubtless useful social function convinced of the impenetrable mysteries of the coincidence of obstinate rocks and the incompetence of the summerfolk.

And how to investigate such an incident? I have the date, I think, in my log, and I could determine, perhaps, which year of the many years I stayed in Boothbay this might have been. And I could check, I suppose, the history of Boothbay, or old newspapers, and somehow I would find out the name of the harbormaster and I could then go, and where would I go? to the Harbor itself to ask about him. And who, do you suppose, would tell me about the arrogant but kindhearted old harbormaster who may have had a distinguished career on the water, but made one stupid and inconsequential mistake that evening?

JACKIE NICHOLS' LOUNGE

One summer before I could legally drink, I played in a band at a bad dance hall on Route 1 somewhere in that area, between, that is, Bath and Boothbay, or perhaps beyond it. The name of the town began with *W,* but there are three of those in that area. Every year, driving up the coast on Route 1, I would see the old dance hall and remember our bad music and our bad band and the bad business of the dance hall, where we had once played, incredibly but justly, to a completely empty house, a detail I recorded as carefully as

I recorded looking for the bow of David's *Tarn* in the fog a
year later. And of course one of those years of driving Route
1, the dance hall was gone, or the road perhaps redirected,
or perhaps it was when Father died and we no longer made
those trips up the coast and I could no longer remember
the pertinent details. When I renewed these drives two
decades later, I could not find the dance hall, and by then
each hill where it used to sit began to look the same, and my
memories of Route 1 began to merge with memories of
driving up Route 1 thinking of earlier drives up Route 1,
and I lost all recollection of where the dance hall was.

I once confused the old dance hall with Moody's Diner
itself, where I asked the waitress who had been there the
longest if she had ever heard of Jackie Nichols' Lounge (or
was it Lodge?); and she replied she had never heard of any
such place and never heard of the ex-wrestler who owned a
dance hall in the area in the '60s and she had grown up
there and drank as a teenager there, and some hell-raiser
she had been! and was older than I was, and there was
nothing in that area she didn't know. So I kept driving,
thinking of the changes in Route 1 itself and driving all the
old roads and trying to remember the phrases from forty
years ago: "Jackie Nichols' Lounge . . ." or was it "Lodge"?
". . . in Wiscasset" or was it "in Woolwich" or was it "in Wal-
doboro"? And how far, driving at hideous speeds in the '60s,
was it compared to how far I drive at the more stately
speeds in the next century? What was it like to drive there
half-drunk as I did then, or sober as I do now? Or to make

my $10 then or spend that much on gasoline today? And which dip in the road was it, or was I remembering instead the dip in the road or the drive to Wiscasset when I spent my first night with Linda Jane at Race's Motel in Boothbay a few years after I willfully forgot about playing bad music in the bad dance hall? And somewhere down there is Bill the harbormaster, now safely feeling his way around Linekin Neck or perhaps still lost and now completely rock-bound and invulnerable in the river.

CHAPTER NINE

PEMAQUID AND MUSCONGUS BAY

When my love swears that she is made of truth,
I do believe her, though I know she lies.

— Shakespeare

MANHATTAN, KANSAS

"Where are you?"

"I'm in . . . I think, Missouri. I'm at a crossroads. One of the roads goes north."

"Which crossroads?"

There is something unnatural about her voice, a hesitation before each reply. She has never given me a studied reply. I assume that is because she is older than I am. We men, I think, always assume our women are more experienced than we are. That is our excuse for most of our ill behavior. I vaguely refer to the highways. One leads west to her house; one leads north to Linda Jane. If I give her the choice of these roads, I will be pretending that our relationship is a small thing, that we have lives of our own, that we can see each other twice a year, when I drive from Maine to California and back. We are sophisticated; our affair, or imagined affair, is simply one inconsequential aspect of our lives. She is more experienced than I, more worldly. But instead of weighing the alternatives, she turns me away.

"I think perhaps you should take the northern road; I think you should stay with your Linda Jane in Nebraska. I think you should not drive here."

When I was introduced to Linda Jane, some months earlier, I could not know the consequences of saying what I said then: Yes, I will stop and visit you where you work in, where is it? is it Nebraska? is it South Dakota? next fall on my way to Los Angeles. I will ignore my affairs in Manhattan (of all names!), Kansas, or my imagined affairs in Kansas. I could not know then that on my way to Los Angeles, I would be told that there were no longer affairs to be pursued in Manhattan, Kansas. There would be no brilliant widow, left there by a suicidal spouse, waiting for me to drive through Kansas twice a year, waiting to play tennis or sit on the porch or talk about dogs and schoolchildren or watch bad movies or play cribbage with her mother in the nursing home. But none of that could possibly be exactly what she said that day.

"Where are you?"

There is a hesitation. Not "how far away" are you or "When could you arrive?" but simply "Where are you?" Am I on the East Coast? Have I perhaps driven straight through? Have I called her repeatedly in the past few weeks promising to visit her? She is more experienced than I; she is not subject to these youthful fluctuations of emotion.

What she says then or what she later says in our last se-
cret meeting in her house in Kansas, hours before I finally
gave up on her and checked into the bad motel in Concor-
dia, what she says is that she has taken up with a farmer
and no longer lives in the house, now overgrown with
brush, where I used to visit her each year. Maine to Los Angeles; Los Angeles to Maine. Beautiful and athletic, wid-
owed by a professor like myself, once producing beautiful
and brilliant children with that professor in Kansas, lovely,
staying there in Manhattan (of all names), Kansas. And why
did she stay once he had so viciously left her there? And
why (so she claims) did she forgive him as her beautiful and
brilliant children could not? And why would she, who could
have any man she wanted in Manhattan, or any one of the
many who must have passed through (a condition, she said,
of agreeing to live there in the first place), why had she
ended up with a failed farmer and a drunk, for whom a
"friend who spends his summers sailing in Maine and stays
with her on his way to California" was a thing, she said,
simply not in his vocabulary, something he could not understand (or was the nuance "could not have understood"?).
Maybe he was a recovering drunk, she said, or maybe she
said alcoholic, as if in wonderment, as everything she said
was in wonderment, a thing that was itself the very wonder
of her, for whom the most trite of banalities could seem so
new and revelatory. She claimed in wonderment she had
never known anyone like that and I told her that was certainly not true. There were too many visitors like me in her

life, too many that she did not know well, and too many of the sort (I imagined) who had left her there in the first place.

But this story is not about her. Not her finding joy there in Kansas with her dead husband and broken-down old farmer of a late lover; not her upbraiding me for my whining and contrived sense of alienation when I first met her. Not about us sleeping in the same room together on the hot August evening in the only cool place in the house in Kansas. It was glorious, was it not? driving from Maine to California? No. This story is not about her, landlocked there in Kansas without a coast within a thousand miles. It is about Linda Jane; it is about being lost, trying to tell a story, a sailing one, no less, about Linda Jane exiled and lost, herself, in the plains of America with her family in some Italian city-state of New Jersey and her adoring husband in Los Angeles.

LOST WITH LINDA JANE

Linda Jane was no real sailor, although I call her one. Her visits to Maine were comical in their duplicity. In those days, there was a single phone in our house, located, with no extension cord, right in the middle of the living room, essentially the only common room of the house. And since the living room was not separated from the kitchen space or dining space, that phone served all those spaces: living room, dining room, and kitchen and everywhere else. That is one of the many ironies of house design for a family whose individual members claimed so vehemently to value their privacies. Father neurotically loved to listen in to the most private of conversations. Mother claimed to resent these, particularly the calls from husbands she was occasionally obliged to take, or, little better, the call from an aging parent, only slightly less galling. She resented me turning to her in the one-room living space while some Linda Jane or other cooed on the phone to her cuckolded husband as I demanded privacy for such cozenings. But Mother was always one to resent the small things and never worry overmuch about the big things—the anguish of the family around her and her own intellectual deterioration, which she steadfastly hid until the end.

That was before electronic navigation was a common thing on the coast of Maine. I never sailed enough in those days to get very good at dead reckoning in the fog. I found the buoys and landmarks I had to find in the fog, and the rest of the time I simply waited it out. I have doubtless been closer to catastrophe with modern navigation instruments than I ever have been without them. Perhaps I should characterize this as "paradoxical," perhaps as "odd." And perhaps I should add "to my knowledge." "To my knowledge," I have been closer to catastrophe. "To my knowledge," I was far safer before modern navigation. Because boating stories, by necessity, are always told of the things that are known or the things that are admitted to be known. What you never hear in sailing stories and what you never see in the authoritative historical and cultural musings of the cruising guides are the things that are not known or the things that are not admitted to be not known.

That unread and uncomposed section of the magazine begins as follows: "Stupidly, despite X, we set sail in . . . and *consequently* lost . . ." "Ignorant as we were of even basic nautical matters and conventions . . ." Instead, what one reads is a tale of heroics, with the mock-deprecation of Tom Wolfe's *The Right Stuff:* "Stupidly [wink], we set sail . . ." and survived on extraordinary strength of character a great adventure.

Imagined adventures as these lead from known to known. Real adventure, by contrast, begins at a single point in the fog and ends at one, and travels of course through unknowns. If I see, by happenstance, a ledge a foot below the keel, or actually hit such a thing, I know or can conclude reasonably that there have been dozens more. I have never missed a buoy completely in the fog, but I have found the wrong one on occasion and I cannot with any certainty explain the courses I took to get there except by guesswork—adverse currents, leeway, a moment's inattention at the helm, a compass error. Finding even the correct buoy in the dense fog is a matter of being lost the entire way—all those minutes of serenity, halfway between marks, when one's position or course do not seem to matter much. When the circle of fog one travels in is sufficient in and of itself. Like finding Linda Jane because some brilliant widow in Kansas had taken up with a lush of a failed farmer. And I said, "OK, I'll take the road to Nebraska north and find a place to stay

there with Linda Jane, and not here in Missouri or Kansas
with you," and she said: "Yes, it's best you see your friend in
Nebraska," where I stayed for weeks.

It was the next summer, or the summer after that, when
Linda Jane and I went sailing on Muscongus Bay.

There were no heroics on this particular sailing trip to
Muscongus and back through Pemaquid. No fabled winds
near fifty and no waves cresting high as the spreaders. I cannot recall where we slept or the physical details that were
the heart, soul, body, and mind of our relationship. I remember the anchor in the fog at Pemaquid with the rode
bent down to the sand. But perhaps that is because that moment is recorded in a morning photograph. And I remember
also coming through Hockomock Channel, in Muscongus
Bay, bound west through that narrowest of passages; even
in those early days of my sailing, we might well have sailed
through it if the wind was right, although it's likely we did
so under mainsail alone with a boost from the diesel. I don't
remember the sound of the engine or the lack of the sound
of the engine. What I remember is the movement of the hull
through the water, south and west through the channel, and
raising the genoa as we passed the last can and feeling the
boat respond to it. As I revise this now, I am struck by a particular and insistent detail in this, my earlier version. It concerns the wind, since in Hockomock Channel, in my
experience, the wind has always been from the south, making for a close and difficult tack. And my memory now of
raising the genoa halfway to that last can is incompatible

with that customary wind from the south. The east wind then, unrecalled, must have been the real wind, or how would we have sailed the ten miles down Muscongus Bay, and how would we have found security in the west-facing bight of Pemaquid?

I remember too, in this my early version, calculating our speed and the distance at Franklin Light in Muscongus Bay the evening before, when we were still bound east. I remember realizing we would not reach the anchorage in Maple Juice Cove by sailing in the remaining daylight. And finally, I can see Linda Jane sick in the vague east wind on the way home as she stuffed the sail into the sailbag, knowing I asked her to do this only to distract her from her seasickness. Those four details of that sail are the only ones I can recall. An anchorage is missing, how the wind was, even what the cruising guide had said, since then, I think, I was limited to Duncan's *Cruising Guide* and the sometimes laughably laconic *United States Coast Pilot,* and how would I have known from these sources that you could sail the inside passage from Friendship to Muscongus through the channel of the Hockomock River, which looks impassable on the charts? Who would have known there was even a road, say, from Glasco, Kansas, to Linda Jane in Nebraska?

LEARNING TO SPEAK

Before Linda Jane, there was little need to speak. You go to school; you listen to television; your eyes see the words lineated on the pages of novels; you forget the plots; you pass tests; there are platitudes of parents; there are the lyrics of bad music. In none of this do you learn to listen or to speak. You do not remember the conversations on even the most momentous of days. Traffic jams. Lights in the rain like Christmas lights. Lying in the back of the old Volvo with a wife-to-be while John drove us through the highways of Connecticut. You see? In those early days, there is just no coherence to such traveling. It is like the bad collage of your best female student. Lost, shall we say, in the sexuality of it all, lost in the hippie embraces of the young wife, you have no reason to speak or to learn how that would be. You style yourself as taciturn, washing your boot soles there cuckolded in Portsmouth. For years I believed in that high taciturnity; until Linda Jane, that is, and until Linda Jane ridiculed that self-delusion as she ridiculed much else.

I say I learned to speak with Linda Jane.

Linda Jane studied Beckett, or modern Irish literature, I think, and her earnest and adoring husband named her two cats (he thought charmingly) Stephen and Leo, which sounded as silly and incomprehensible to Linda Jane herself as it did to most she told the story to. Was it some allusion to lions? she claimed to have thought. And, adoring though the husband was, who would think of burdening a cat with a formal name like Stephen? When she sailed, she sailed with the same enthusiasm with which she cooked and with which she drove (so badly!), since in these matters, there was really nothing at stake for her. She could be ill, and look through the fog, and throw the chart away, because her sailing had nothing to do with her relationship to me, and we, whoever "we" were, would proceed regardless, as we did regardless of, say, husbands, and thousands of intervening miles, and weekend trips on Western Airlines, where I would sit, I imagined, in the seat warmed by her husband on his way back to Los Angeles. Moving through the water on the boat, past the recalcitrant tides of, say, Seguin, into the opposing flow of the St. George River, nothing mattered but her speaking to me: I am Linda Jane. I am Linda Jane. Learning to speak with Linda Jane meant learning to say such things, just as learning to love, years earlier, with my wife, yes, as John drove through the Hartford of Wallace Stevens and the Danbury of Charles Ives, meant learning to address the peculiarities of the line past her shoulder to her waist, and realizing, as we all finally must, that there was nothing really unique about that most unique of lines from her shoulder to her waist.

It was that, I think, that finally freed me of my contrived marriage vows, vows which meant nothing in the first place, and took me back to my working on the water, somehow lost in the small and line-confined working area of the lobster boat or in my own inabilities to master single-handed sailing or in the days when all went well on the water.

Past Franklin Island in the early evening, Linda Jane finally marvels at the quiet wake of the boat through the water, through the easy ebbing flow of the St. George River. The distance to the cove is eight miles. The speed through the water is four knots, and over ground somewhat less

than that. Under the best of circumstances, it will take two
hours just to reach the anchorage. There is less time than
that to sunset. Linda Jane is amazed at the calculation. We
are moving better than we have moved all day.

The water is clear; the lighthouse glides by as she turns
to speak; the air explodes in the grinding of the diesel.

There is nothing I recall of the nights, no jokes that the
swells rocking us at the anchorage were really from our
rocking of the boat itself, none, say, about the landlord's
power tools, which Linda Jane's neighbors mistook for
sewing and which we pretended was the sound of a sex toy.
No allusions, say, to the dorm room at some college in New
Jersey, where we had met on the pretense of grading the Advanced Placement essays of ambitious sixteen-year-olds. I
cannot recall where in the boat we slept, even in that cabin
with so few options, or what we said, or the details of her
flesh or her breath, or trying to take what constituted
a shower, or eating dinner or waking, or the night sky, or
any of the picturesque details through which I could describe it, such as, "while the fog drifted over the black night
sky . . ." And I think that's what I miss most about Linda
Jane. I do not care much for the pain of it nor have I ever
been embarrassed by the absurdly contrived assignations.
But the heart of it seems gone to me, returning only, and
strangely, during the most inapt of times. It is the opera,
this time, reviled by her as the epitome of aristocratic deca-
dence. *Tristan,* I think, twenty years since I have seen her. So
dark it is in the music, alone there, in the balcony. And

Linda Jane suddenly fills the darkness of the hall as she once filled my life.

On that ridiculous trip to Princeton, even the rankest moralist must admire her. It takes a particular agility of mind to tell your husband you are flying to Princeton from Los Angeles in order to spend a week grading Advance Placement exams, reading the endless essays with their jejune moralizing on the same jejune questions, like the worst of sailing magazines. "From my earliest childhood, in the fog, I have always known, sailing past Bimini . . ." I sneaked, for the first time in my life, into a women's dorm for her, or didn't really "sneak" there, since there were no regulations then such as there likely were in my day, and certainly not for the residents in summer programs, it being moot in such pious times to regulate a behavior one can't foresee occurring: "Item: There will be no smuggling of one's cuckolding lovers into the single-sex dormitory floors."

I can still see the startled face of the middle-aged English teacher in her unflattering teddy, thinking how grand it was to be in Princeton, magical Princeton, even if it was only Rider College next to Princeton. In her teddy from who knows where in the dry and sealess Midwest, doing the Business of Education, real education. Here, in this academic land, while her colleagues back home painted houses and de-tasseled the cornfields, now, here, in all the glory of teaching now for real instead of just pretending to, these two unknowns, thumbing their noses at the true Business of Education, followed their base desires like some high school kids, sneaking glimpses of midwestern schoolteachers in their unflattering nightwear. And again, lost there in Rider College, although I remember the face of the woman in her outlandish teddy, I cannot remember the love and pain that must have been in Linda Jane's face as we lay together. I think instead of the cheap convention hotel room in San Francisco when we knew it was the last time; and it was like that trail in the San Gabriels, just north of Los Angeles, your killing call from Bonnie Avenue, or posing for the camera that fall day on Monhegan.

Someone should write a play about us teachers. No one knows how hard life is for us.
                                        —*Chekhov,* The Seagull

One of the few moments of high anxiety all teachers experience is the first class, whether that is the first of each new year or the first of one's career. I maintain this anxiety, perhaps as a tribute to my first taste of it, just as, I suppose, sailing in the gentlest of rains, I still long for that first experience, crossing the Muscongus with Linda Jane all done up in her outsized raingear.

I am in graduate school, and the first class I am scheduled ever to teach is tomorrow. So I lay my hand-me-down denim jacket on the chair, the jacket with the *Rockford Files* lapels and visible stitching, and my tie is there and maybe the garishly striped shirt I had worn the day before just to get used to it. I think my father once wore these; but he was still alive in those days, so the costume must have been dated even by his standards if they were then in my possession. I awoke (if I had ever slept), and despite that preparation, "Damn!" I could not find my carefully selected tie. Not on the chair, not on the floor, not inadvertently moved to the bathroom. A tie was the one article of clothing that in those days had to remain between all teachers and their students. And now it had disappeared. By some unwitting prescience (perhaps I knew a story would later be told), I owned another tie; so I grabbed it, put it on, tied it, with surprising expertise, and ran across what I'll call a quad in my *Rockford Files* jacket and striped shirt and creased pants to my first class. I stood there nervously in front of five students and waited for the room to fill up and it never did beyond those five bright and docile freshmen. It was twenty minutes into class before I realized I was wearing two ties.

This was a tale I told many times to Linda Jane, and she never tired of hearing my most recent variation.

And now I am dreaming. This is the perfect place for it. The dream is a variant of the dream all academics dream— the one where we search for the examination room of the course we have forgotten to attend all semester. "Oh my God!" the young instructor, reading this, can be counted on to say. "Oh my God I too have . . ." Everyone who teaches has the dream. In this version, I am walking across (again what I will call) the quad of the small college I attended and where my father taught in his nervous ebullience. I am on my way to lecture on Carolingian history, and despite the legal pad of notes I am carrying I know that I know nothing of Carolingian history, nor do I suspect, then, that this whole historical period might be a convoluted variant of the name of my sister. I desperately imagine that if I can just find the transition to, say, the twelfth-century feudal system, I will be fine, until I realize I know little about that subject either, although one of my yellow legal sheets has scattered and indecipherable notes on Georges Duby's *mentalités*.

At this point, I see that I am wearing a costume from, say, *The Rockford Files* again, or better yet, Scorsese's *Goodfellas*. A yellow polyester shirt, open at the chest. Too small, with the sleeves rolled up once. I may be missing the gold chain, I suppose. My pants are white, and thin, and tight, so tight and thin there is no possibility, I realize, of relieving myself before class.

I consider: I have two options. I can simply brazen it out: I am not merely playing at being a college professor; like my father, I truly am one. I can confidently go in and lecture away, and be damned and damn the students if they speak of my polyester shirts or peculiar ties. Or I can ironize my way out of it; we are all mere players here, I'll assert, students and professors and auditors alike: "I am certain, gentlemen, you find it as amusing as I do that I am here in this preposterous costume, over which, of course, I choose to have no control." Lost in these thoughts, I enter the building where my father had his office, and whose unique smells still take me back to sitting in that office as a seven-year-old, drawing pictures of schooners. Somewhere on the shelves is an intricately compartmented wooden box with white and black marbles, which he claimed was some kind of Roman, I think, voting machine, and I suppose this explains in some way the term "blackball." And that is likely why, in the dream, now that I am late to class in my yellow shirt from *Goodfellas*, a voice cries out, "Joe! You need to vote."

I tell you this story, Linda Jane, because you so loved that other one. But here I am still lost, searching for your face in my hands, about which I claim to have once written so eloquently. All I find are the studied blank intimidated faces of those five freshmen, the woman in the teddy, the wooden voting box from my father's office, the rain on the sail as the boat sails past the buoys of Muscongus on different years and different trips, and the precise calculations of time and distance that ended in the engine roar at Franklin Light.

Months after she was gone I wrote to her, and I received back two letters on consecutive days, the first like the long and intricate letters she once delivered through our pandering friends, and the second note, merely a Post-it, saying simply: "We cannot be friends. Please do not write or call."

Years later, I wrote her again, or more accurately, I sent an e-mail, since I kept no record of her address there in California. I told her of meeting a once-mutual friend at the Frick gallery in New York—oh yes another aristocratic institution, so she would have scoffed, and I laughed at how she would have said this. I got back a note from her and it reminded me of a line I wrote in some verse to her she never read. In Verdi's *Rigoletto*, Gilda is murdered because her father, the court jester Rigoletto, has stupidly set a trap to kill the Duke, who has seduced her. But the would-be murderer's sister begs the would-be murderer Sparafucile (if I have this right) to spare the Duke and kill instead the first person who comes to the inn, and that turns out to be Gilda, looking for the Duke. Sparafucile then cuts Gilda's throat, stuffs her into a bag, and he and his sister hand the whole business over to Rigoletto.

Do they expect the poor jester to be deceived by this? Even if he tosses the bag into the river, won't he discover everything the next day at the ducal court? But this is not worrisome onstage, where all takes place, and Rigoletto learns of this savage trickery right in front of us as he hears the Duke singing *La donna è mobile* . . . from the upstairs window of the inn. And what can he do but open the bag and there he finds his daughter Gilda with her throat cut . . .

Why does it take so long to tell these simplest of things? The point is, getting her throat cut is apparently no big deal; Gilda delivers her final aria regardless. And I wrote then, though changing the execution mode for the very euphony of it: "Garroted by Sparafucile, she still sang . . ."

It is difficult to remember the precise words in the note I got back from Linda Jane, having learned that I had seen her old friend in the Frick, and difficult too to recall the melody of Gilda's aria. It is like losing your way in the fog in the complex web of times and positions you have logged with a china marker on the chart. So I will tell you I got back a final note from Linda Jane—oh how nice to have met Jan and thank you so much for sending me news of him, I was always so fond of him, and it's so good to know he is doing well . . . And one day I finally composed these lines and I think I actually wept for Linda Jane as I wrote:

Garroted by Sparafucile, she still sang.
It was as if nothing had happened.
It was as if there had been no grand debaucheries.

PART IV

THE
PENOBSCOT AND
MOUNT DESERT

CHAPTER TEN

THE WEST
PENOBSCOT

Holding traffic for Linda Jane.

Camden Marine operator

Linda Jane, young and beautiful, reads while lying prone on the cushion, her knees bent and her feet kicked up in a pose I associate with the 1950s—*Lolita*, was it? a cigarette ad? She was disturbed only by losing sight of land in the haze of the West Penobscot as we sailed over from Owl's Head to Hurricane Sound, in the middle of Vinalhaven Island. At the south end of that sound is Hurricane Island, the offshore anchorage and name-place of the Hurricane Island Outward Bound School, with its humorless, militaristic counselors and teenaged crews. Ignoring them, we drift with the incoming tide on the glacial surface of the sound, south to north, straight to Long Cove, where Joshua Slocum was said to have stayed a century ago.

Linda Jane and I will continue sailing with the tide out of the north end of the sound, through Leadbetter's Narrows and into the Fox Island Thoroughfare, which separates the islands of North Haven and Vinalhaven. In Waterman Cove, the worst possible disturbance will be merely the music that occasionally drifts across the island from the secure Pulpit Harbor cutting into the land from the north shore, a harbor now filled with anchored boats and moorings.

Linda Jane has demanded a shower. And tomorrow, we will sail to the North Haven wharf and tie up somehow and go ashore. This shower, always hers, became briefly a tradition as I struggled in later years to remember this trip with Linda Jane. All the establishments on North Haven that supported it are now different establishments or they are boarded shut. When I went ashore with Linda Jane, it was, I recall, a Sunday morning when everything was closed and we had to slide under the doors of the shower stalls and leave the money, or pretend to, under the doorway at Waterman's Store. Or that may have been a later sail and it may not have been Linda Jane at all. It was there, on the door to the store or perhaps in the stolen shower room, that I first saw the Peter Ralston print, now famous as these things go, of a dory full of sheep, towed by a large green dragger, headed through the fog for Mr. Ralston to play Maine on Allen Island.

It's been years since I've stopped in North Haven, and Linda Jane is now doubtless a version of her unsmiling, large-breasted mother. The wide and empty wharf, set parallel to the shore and so easy to approach, even under sail, is gone, and you have to motor your way into the narrow and inconvenient fingers of the wharfs of J. O. Brown & Son. The winds are always quiet and my only goal now is to sail as the cruising boats motor past, inevitably bound east, no matter which way I am heading. Bound east, I hope to make it past the moored boats and through the narrows to the solitude of Waterman or Kent Cove. Bound west, always in the early morning, I hope for a minimum of fog in the western entrance, with Brown's Head just visible and the alternate passages free past Dogfish Rock and the red spindle at its northern end. There is sometimes time and the proper tide conditions to revisit Hurricane Sound and think of Linda Jane reading, or Linda Jane setting the anchor at the north end of the small island in the entrance to Slocum's Long Cove.

Bound east or bound west, Linda Jane will always rule this place. Linda Jane, self-sufficient and undemanding, wanting nothing more than a shower for her hair. She became a lawyer and must have lost her stunning girlishness, although I never saw that, nor can I now imagine it. Waterman's Store on North Haven where we took and stole those showers—its cascade of tiny rooms with their sundries in some barely discernible order—Waterman's Store mentioned in all the cruising guides, Waterman's Store was a must-see and now it's gone. You don't need to look for Corn Flakes, I suppose, on the island when you can buy them cheap in Rockland and bring them over on the ferry, running full-throttle in the fog across the cruising lanes in the West Penobscot.

In the poster on the unknown wall in North Haven, the dory is still full of tethered sheep bound for Allen Island. But Allen Island has changed, due in part to the events alluded to in the poster, as the Island Institute tries to return the island to the productive state it enjoyed in the late nineteenth century, when it, like so many islands on the Maine coast, was used as a convenient and predator-free grazing area for sheep. This state of things, whether now or a century ago, was attained by clear-cutting those stands of fir as ruthlessly as the worst real estate investor might do today. That traditional Maine, with all its trees ground up in houses and firewood, was spared the fate of deserts only by the institution of oil and electric power, which themselves do not figure much in tales of traditional Maine, unless it is in the muted diesels of the offshore fishing boats, or the less muted oil-fired generator on Matinicus Island.

If the old photographs speak the truth, barely a tree stood in my own neighborhood of South Harpswell at the turn of the century, and the entrance to the Basin and its dozens of houses was controlled by the gristmill placed at the entrance. All that stood then were the bad and airless houses heated by the fires of the devastated fir. Why restore this state of things? Didn't Linda Jane herself leave with barely a word of protest? And didn't I watch her go without feeling? Was playing Maine in those days something new, foreign? Brought in, perhaps, by the steamers from Boston while the Maine people themselves (as Maine people were then) laid waste to the landscape in their efforts to survive the winter?

Linda Jane is a partner now. Or she left the law. Or she married a drunkard and got fat and bored raising her children. I wonder if she thinks of me and if the me she dreams of is as young as she will always be young when I dream of her. She walks slowly down the old staircase in the guest cottage; she wears an orange bathing suit that could not be less appropriate for the early July waters in the bay. Seeing her once dressed like that, the dock attendant at the marina was struck dumb and called me "Mr. Dane" for the rest of the summer. And there she stands as if modeling that suit for my approval, but the desire overwhelmed me and overwhelms me still today. We throw ourselves on the cot downstairs, and momentarily forget our families, her sullen large-breasted mother, the remnant taciturnity of my own, the gay blades leering from the old photographs. We ignore the stupidity of my knowing that I would leave her, or that she would grow up bored with me, or find some drunkard to abuse her.

Linda Jane was rarely defeated, growing up as she had somewhere in the Great Plains among broken families and tornado warnings. She was never bothered by such things as car accidents, infidelities, the errors of errant and unskilled sailors. I see her walking through the silver light of the supermarket, after I had quashed her enthusiasm for Thanksgiving by refusing to prepare for her this all-too-American meal. As in a scene from Herzog's *Stroszek,* she is carrying in her arms a ten-pound turkey as if it were a child. I must show her this film, I think, and she will one day claim Herzog is her favorite director. And this is long before *Grizzly Man*, of course, or *Incident at Loch Ness*.

And why restore this state of things? She held me the hardest when she knew I would let her go. "I was always such a happy person," she says, meaning, I suppose, that I had done something to destroy that. My affairs, my leaving her for Maine, my very solicitude. Do the years that I have thought about her restore any of that to her? What have I held of her? when what I hold is not my beloved Linda Jane, but my memory of her, strong and beautiful in my arms?

Wade, young, gay, black, sits next to me with a later Linda Jane, young as well, slim and desperately depressed, who would die of self-medication within the year. Wade sits with me absurdly in an all-white hockey arena, talking of the Lakers. He is protective of everyone he knows, even of Linda Jane, who with her taut profile leaned forward watches the skaters with unusual attention, as if she knows she will never watch these men again. We are landlocked, here in the artificial ice of Southern California, and Wade, I suggest, should visit me to integrate also those harbors of southern Maine. We persuade the two Finns with us, researchers at the Huntington, to help us shout encouragement to Teemu Selanne, but perhaps this is a different night in Anaheim I remember.

Wade has misplaced her address, or maybe we have simply forgotten it. Linda Jane has moved. She has lapsed back into her family, in California, New York, Kansas again, or Alaska. She is done with sailing. She has changed her name and is now unfindable in any of these places. She will never kick her feet up in a pose from the 1950s again. Wade shakes his head: "Damn!" he says, as Linda Jane yells suddenly: "Kill the bastards!" You attend such season-ending games as this, she says, interrupting us, only for the perfunctory fights. In such season-ending games, there can be no consequences, no changes in playoff positions. Just penalty minutes, Linda Jane continues, barely heard, and, with luck, some sports esoterica. "And she *loved* you!" Wade says, ignoring this. "For some damn reason, that woman *loved* you." Still solicitous of her, even to the end.

CAMDEN MARINE, CHANNEL 28

One of the great pleasures of playing Maine in what I will one day call the old days was the Camden Marine operator. You could tune to Camden Marine Radio on Channel 28 of the then-standard VHF. Before cell phones made even the illusion of solitude impossible, you made calls through a shoreside operator, who, here on land, would dial the call and end with "Have a good evening," after you had played Maine by saying "Over" at each phrase, just like in the movies, or, for someone my age, just like Broderick Crawford on the old black-and-white TV series *Highway Patrol*.

The calls were not cheap; I paid $5 for the last one. But the calls you made were not the sole benefits of the marine operator; Channel 28, like all channels on VHF, was completely open. And on a foggy night, you could tune to 28 and listen, call after call: "Holding traffic for the *L.J.*" "Thank you Camden, this is . . . out." You listened mostly to ordinary sailors like myself, calling home, calling a relative who had opened the summerhouse for them, a daughter, a shore mechanic, calling an envious and still-working friend in Massachusetts. There were occasional commercial fishermen calling home, although most of them, of course, could be heard on other open frequencies of the VHF talking to each other directly. When the calling boat was distant, only the operator's voice could be heard, and sometimes Camden Marine itself would go silent: "You're breaking up . . . Come back." And you would piece together the conversation amid the curiosities of boat names, *Sceptre,* the *Dawnela, Classics XII,* and *Hawke II* itself. The operator's voice was always soporific and assuring, and what could be amiss or threatening if one could speak that way? Hers was a voice like that of the famed Art Lester, who read the NOAA weather in coastal Maine and speaks for the last time later in this book. But hers was a voice without his ironies. "Camden Marine, holding traffic for Linda Jane"; "Camden Marine, come back."

It is evening and I am near sleep in the candlelight, in the stylized, staged sonorities of Channel 28. All know we are listening, and as a result, the worst of days become great sailing days, each sailor and landsman much missed. A lover ignores the open-channel VHF and proclaims to the entire coast of Maine her now-public lust. In the sailor's morphean attention, all slows to drawled understatement, to studied calm ". . . Well . . . it was . . . uh . . . brisk . . . we'll . . . uh . . . be in . . . oh . . . well . . . tomorrow . . . Think. Yup . . . uh . . . 'n . . . Over." What Maine are we playing? And is the crackle and squelch of Camden Marine and the breathy calm of the operator a constant that the actual sailing days themselves cannot provide?

In *The Right Stuff,* Tom Wolfe talks of the required accent of pilots, modeled on Chuck Yeager. I am on Air India, flying into London on my first and sleepless overseas flight. The pilot, in an Indian accent as thick as my father's Maine, larded over now with a desperate Chuck Yeager, announces: "This . . . uh . . . is your py-lott speaking . . . Uh . . . We will be . . . uh . . . landing in Manchester. [Yeager pause]. There is . . . [Yeager "uh"] . . . fog in Heathrow and . . . uh . . . we have a . . . uh . . . little fire in the baggage compartment."

The last two years of the marine operator, things changed. There was a jamming mechanism that the operator used to block the inadvertent relaying of a caller's credit card number. And soon, that jamming mechanism must have been perfected; one June, I tuned to Channel 28 and there were no more calls to listen to. Calls were routed through a company called MariTEL in Gulfport, near New Orleans, whose operator had the wrong accent and no idea of the weather conditions that evening in Maine and didn't know Port Clyde from Petit Manan; and around the same time came the cell phone, and the Camden Marine operator and all she brought us was gone for good.

It is ridiculous to speak of such institutions and the accidents that befell them with nostalgia, for listening in to the marine operator was a self-indulgent and likely illegal thing to do. The tradition I imagined could only have existed a decade or so, when the exigencies of telephones permitted it. Like the sleek sloop hull sailing efficiently in the ten-knot afternoon breeze, the ornamented cottage on a deserted hill in Kennebunk.

SAIL PLANS

Linda Jane sails with me always on the end of this trip, and always bound west. I find her in the early morning on the town dock in Rockland, as the weather warms in late June. She has bags of provisions and freshly grown strawberries from her garden—fresh greens, rain gear, even a sun shower one year, clean silverware. We stow all this, and one year at 10 AM caught the gentlest of breezes that took us silently from the dock, through the moored boats, and into the clear and flat surface of Rockland Harbor. "This is heaven," she said. "This is heaven."

That heaven, fraudulent though it was, was all I could provide for her, out there paired in what seemed the inevitable shape of the boat. That space held none of the adverse socialities of life—her job and children, my coast-to-coast meandering and part-time Maine-playing. All that grand philandering! It was heaven, she said, because it was an allusion like heaven is. It was like sailing in the preposterously appropriate design of a modern fiberglass yacht, appropriate, that is, for the bourgeois lifestyle of vacation, of work and rest, of nostalgia, technology, and New England weather conditions. All obscured in the delusion of Maine and playing Maine as we briefly enjoy heaven on a straight tack from Rockland through the West Penobscot to the south shore of Vinalhaven.

Before Linda Jane taught me about boat design, I often marveled that the temperance of weather conditions in the Northeast and in the world generally permits exactly the kind of single-handed sailing I do and the ordinary year-round commercial sailing of the eighteenth and nineteenth centuries. Suppose, I would muse, the average wind velocity in Maine summers were thirty knots instead of ten. Suppose the variation in wind speed on an average summer day were forty knots. Where would our great sailing days be then?

Yet this is like the delusional wonder of the universe itself—a wonder still expressed in popular simile-laden geological histories you will find, say, on Amazon. There is plenty to wonder about in the world of art and literature and science. But not in amateur yachting. And not in rock formations. The details of yachting are a function of man's evolving intolerance for suffering. Had sea conditions been like those I've read of in the North Atlantic, or around the southern 40s, the graceful particulars of a modern sailing yacht would be unknown. We would be driven around our shores in bathysphere-like objects, lovely, we would say, tethered, perhaps, to port or to distant moorings, propelled by an as-yet-undiscovered way of harnessing salinity variations. And the same "true sailors" would still exist and cruise and seem all salty and would marvel at the remarkable coincidence of their tethered bathyspheres and the perfectly appropriate conditions in which they sailed. Perhaps they would become theological about the entire thing.

All boat design, Linda Jane explained, hull shape, sail design and area, keel, proportions, size of cabin, skid surfaces on decks—all these are desperate and long-evolving responses to what is simply there. This is why the confrontation with "what is usually not there" is so traumatic for small coastal sailing boats like mine and coastal sailors like myself. Gales, breaking waves on normal passageways, lightning—any kind of abnormality—something out of the normal experience. One must confront these liminalities without doing so in a threatening or dangerous way.

Linda Jane, sailing out of Rockland, is trapped in that boat design. She is trapped in the bourgeois structure that grew up around "what is there." Her own boat is exactly that design, and the two of us sail in an eerie repetition of a sail of thirty years ago, from Belfast to Harpswell in the late summer. Only this time there is no grand drama, no offshore storm, no anxieties of anchoring. It is all so routine, recorded in photographs from carefully packed cameras, and meals planned and prepared in the rain, and the GPS ready for use if necessary. The fog lifts at Port Clyde, where even Waterman's Store in North Haven seems reborn in the rambling grocery rooms; and it is a straight run to Pemaquid, with only a small break for the conversation we have agreed not to have that day. Linda Jane on the sail to Pemaquid; Linda Jane on the way to the St. George River; Linda Jane meeting the boat in Rockland, or wrapping her arms around my waist on a daysail around Haskell Island near Harpswell.

I am in the Penobscot, but I write this lying on a soulless rented mooring in Northeast Harbor, well to the east, as a two-day gale, so like the one of twenty years ago, blows overhead.

CHAPTER ELEVEN

STONINGTON

When I dream, it's you I dream of.

—Linda Jane

You leave the Penobscot through the Deer Island Thorofare, insistently distinct in its spelling from its counterpart Fox Islands Thoroughfare cutting between Vinalhaven and North Haven, and soon you will be out of range of the Camden Marine operator and Down East.

Stonington is the only working harbor you will pass and itself the last town on the road from Orland south through Deer Isle. The large sign "Opera House" dominates the landscape from the sea. Stonington has all that is required for the guidebooks to describe it as an authentic fishing village. The same thing was doubtless said about Camden a few decades ago, and Boothbay Harbor before that and likely Kennebunk, where I nearly lost my boat on the first day out. You can still see fishermen urinate off the docks and you can still walk on the streets and be mocked by local kids in fishing gear driving past in pickup trucks. My jeans and beard and even my voice do me no good here, where I am instantly identified as summerfolk.

I often confuse this harbor with Friendship in Muscongus Bay, also authentic in the best and worst of ways,
where the fishermen, unique on the coast, I think, do not return your wave. There, the spot once good to anchor in is
now filled with the moored wharfs of the fishermen of
Friendship, who have sold off their shorefront property and
now have access to the water only by the grace of the company or community that owns the working wharf. It is only
a matter of time before the same moored wharfs appear at
Stonington.

At Stonington, the schooners from Camden and Rockland still anchor off the islands south of the Thorofare and
north of the passage known as Merchant's Row. You can
sail through the Thorofare, although in light air you will
likely find yourself becalmed on the western edge near
Billings Marine. In the ordinary southwesterlies of the late
afternoon, you will be blown past Stonington in less than an
hour.

Tides are important here. Oriented east-west, the channel should produce an easterly flow during the flood tide, a
westerly flow during the ebb. But its force and direction,
guidebooks claim, depend on factors too complex to be predicted, and from what I know they are correct. I routinely
calculate the logic of tides as I sail through, considering
its moon-fed ebb and flood and how that flow will help or
hinder me. Yet the June tide in the Thorofare aligns itself
with the usual southwest wind and thus both sets and ebbs
to the east, and it does so with particular ferocity in the late

afternoon when you are trying to beat west from Jericho Bay.

You can bypass Stonington altogether by sailing south among the islands forming Merchant's Row, or farther south between those islands and the large mass of Isle au Haut. Or you can sail well north and take the inside route north of Deer Isle through Eggemoggin Reach, where a few years ago the dude schooner was flattened by an autumn gust. You will sail there beneath the bridge that is a sister to the Tacoma Narrows Bridge, which famously collapsed months after it opened in 1940 in a video we have all seen many times. If you sail that way, and it is still midseason, you will pass the abandoned marina where the sole boat moored is the catboat once owned by my father. Here is where my brother plays at playing Maine in a white clapboard house on Little Deer Isle just past the precarious bridge, where he can put in his kayaks from his own backyard and Father's boat is just a mile away. He has become exactly the kind of lawyer you would want to have, and neither of us is entirely happy with the fact that it is I who get credit for being "just like Dad." Quite early in life, he directed his own version of Father's high obsessions toward correcting the inadequacies of traditional baseball statistics. Others, we all know, have now made millions doing the same thing, listening, as he did, to every Red Sox game in the summer and unraveling the mysteries of their then-spare virtues.

WILDLIFE

Duncan's *Cruising Guide* is one of the few guides to contain no section on any of the natural things one might encounter on the Maine coast—nothing about the birds, fish, or mammals, nothing about the firs and forest succession, little to nothing about the weather itself. Perhaps in those days it just seemed that exotic birds and whales would be with us as long as the Labrador current from the melting ice cap produced the Down East fogs. My family had different notions about these things, and it was only the abstruse chemistry of the Krebs cycle that kept me from pursuing my interest in the newts breeding in a neighbor's pond and living my then-inevitable future as a biologist.

Although a guiltless killer of shrikes, my father kept an obsessively correct record of first-sightings of bird species for each year. As I read through his record book, I note with interest the missing years: a two-year span in the 1950s and a short stretch in the mid-1970s. I believe the first gap is what I call the "owser" years, when Mother kept us quiet by referring to Father's terror of "ulcers." The second gap is likely a consequence of moving to Harpswell, where, with their children grown, both Mother and Father claimed for some reason "there just were no birds," even though this spring I spotted a Townsend's solitaire, that rarest of all things in this region, on Potts Point.

In Father's six-by-nine-inch, three-ringed notebook, each bird species has its own page, and on each page is a series of dates—the first day of each year in which that species was seen, beginning in 1935. The sequence of pages, I think, reflects simply the order in which those birds were first seen and recorded. When he saw what he termed a "life species," he would add a new page.

There are two indexes. The first is in my father's hand and is in the order of species as they are presented in Peterson's classic *Field Guide to Birds*. Unless you are a skilled ornithologist, that index is hardly more useful than the seemingly random order of pages in the book itself. The second index, incomplete, is by my mother. This is alphabetized, although there are problems with compound names like "great blue heron," or "solitary sandpiper," which are not entirely worked out. Father could, of course, have used the ringed notebook to advantage, rearranging its leaves in any order he wanted. But early in life, he must have decided to save paper by entering species both on the recto and verso, that is (as I carefully instruct my students), by page rather than by leaf—a poor decision with obvious consequences still reflected in the labored indexes.

Family man as he imagined himself to be, Father had on the opening page crossed out the first word of the title MY BIRDS and written, in equally imposing and to me familiar capitals, OUR. Better, in 1942, to emphasize the act of performing this familial piety than to construct a new title page altogether. Mother herself kept her (or was it "their"?) parallel record in a different system in a diary, beginning the year she bought us all diaries for Christmas, and I, for a year or two, wrote when I could "Saw Linda Jane," meaning I had caught a glimpse of her as her class walked past the windows to my classroom on their way to lunch. I am not certain whether Mother's diary is collated with Father's records, nor how she would know on, say, May 24th, whether she had or had not seen a magnolia warbler earlier in the year. Perhaps she checked ~~MY~~ OUR BIRDS for that.

In the late 1970s, there is erratic activity in the bird books, including a two-year gap and a renewed calculation of the number of species seen each year. This is done with serenity, since the annual species then identified by them, now near retirement and old by the standards of that generation, hardly competed with those seen in the glory days of the 1950s. Then occurred what Mother termed in some phone conversation I overheard the "calamity" or "catastrophe" of Father's death—a word that seemed inapt to me then. And there it is again.

A lapse. A renewal.

The entries in the book begin again, now in my mother's hand. They are confined to ~~MY~~ OUR BIRDS, a book that the handwriting suggests she had never used earlier. Even the half-finished index is likely contemporary with the entries from the 1980s. My own version of this book, whose pages are more coherently arranged in Peterson order, also shows a halting renewal during these years. But I never had Father's ornithological skills; too many of my entries are doubtfuls. And like Mother, I could never bring myself to "go birding"—to wake up early and seek these birds out in some distant location like Merrymeeting Bay. They must come to me, and the only place I have my Peterson guide at hand is on my boat. I imagine the loose-leafed notebooks of my brother and sister also have memorial entries for those years in the early 1980s. And I imagine too, like mine, like Mother's, these simply fade out.

Reduced to such playing at birding, rather than really doing it, we must settle for the half tribute, half memorial of our mere associations. I always associate Brother with his scissor-tailed flycatcher, which he actually saw, and (for some reason) the razor-billed auk, which he claims only to have seen in books; Mother with her favorite bluebird, the gray-cheeked thrush, the night heron, and the yellow-billed cuckoo, whose "behavior" she often remarked upon.

Sailing now through Stonington, the list I construct for this trip is no longer confined to birds. I will have seen by now most of what I expected: the common profligates of puffins and more subtle auk, the magnificent gannets, known (at least by name) to Old English poets of more than a millennium ago, either the minke or the finback whale, which, despite their differences in size, are indistinguishable when they break the surface, and the sunfish, hundreds of pounds, barely mobile, drifting with the fin flopping on the surface. Its sexual habits, I read, are ill understood.

There are jellyfish, themselves preyed upon by sunfish, I read, whose categories of red/white, poisonous/harmless we were incorrectly assured were analogous. And the few fish I know as game—mackerel, tuna, striped bass. Most saltwater fish I can identify are groundfish, and I know them only from the bait barrel—brim, imported from Nova Scotia, or the "dragged bait" of haddock, hake, whiting. I think of John, playing Maine by fishing in the still ponds of the North Woods, and I think of Linda Jane, choosing the wrong metaphor for me and admonishing me, for perhaps the last time, "No more. The catch-and-release routine is done." The terns gather in the distance. There are years that meant bluefish, and sport fishermen slaughtered them by the hundreds, while claiming wrongly they were inedible. I killed mine, caught under sail with a hand line, in the cockpit, slashing with the utility knife while I stood ankle-deep in blood, much of it my own, trying to keep the cushions and the mainsheet clean.

KAYAKS OF WEBB COVE

I have stopped at the wharf in Stonington itself only once. The delay then put me just outside Pickering Cove, square in the path of a thundersquall, with its classic and terrifying roll cloud, engulfed in such impenetrable rain the only thing visible were the lightning strikes. Like struggling with a bluefish in the cockpit, it is something I am content to have done once. Since then, I take photographs of the large "Opera House" sign as I pass.

There are relatives in and about that place, but it is difficult to arrive anywhere on schedule under sail. The water, I pretend to think, is not a harbor but a passage, this most authentic harbor on the coast (or what was once that). Right off the wharfs at Stonington, as those at Port Clyde or Jonesport—these are not grounds I have the gear to anchor in although the dude schooners often do. It is as if the string of buoys, east and west, can be known only by their numbers and the placement on the chart, marking that course, east and west.

For the best anchorage in Stonington, you need to sail out of your way north, say, to Billings Cove or Pickering Cove, or work deep into the island itself to the protected water of Southeast Harbor. There is a single more convenient anchorage right off the Thorofare at Webb Cove, whose water is both calm and too shallow for the schooners to disturb you. It is also the put-in spot for summer kayakers, and you cannot sail this area without meeting them. Linda Jane thus appears beside me as I sail at half-hull speed through the Thorofare in the light fog. She maneuvers her bright kayak more closely, paddling quietly in the undisturbed surface. She asks for food. She asks this slowly, with a well-practiced and unhurried accent. It is unimaginable to me why she does this. I offer her dinner instead, sailing easily in the current and the unperplexing air. Webb Cove, too shallow for the schooners, is somewhere nearby, just beyond Grog Island, with its modern, but unassuming, summer home. I point through the light fog to this imagined anchorage a half mile or more in the distance, and it may well be where she herself began this trip. I will be there within the hour. She can watch me anchor, so picturesque in my Grundéns, in the soft and unthreatening fog. But she persists. She has no time for this, she says, speaking so serenely. How can she be hungry, and how can she expect me to provide for her? I go below. The boat sails easily, maintaining its course in the light air. I toss her a box of saltines. You really can't provision too many of these, I say. She glides off wakeless into the fog.

CHAPTER TWELVE

SWAN'S ISLAND

*You're from California, ain't you? I had your
mother for high school.*

—Local fisherman

In my family, no one really learned to speak. Mother lying
in her nursing home. Series of strokes. TIAs, the nurses call
them, for "transient ischemic attacks," but they are strokes.
It is absolutely not the case that they leave you undamaged,
as one of my woods-living friends very deliberately testifies.
They give her Valium, to calm her down I guess. Losing
more between each visit in the assuaging tones of the
nurses. Sense of irony gone; then the narratives; then the
sentences. She waves her hand to push away the irritations.
I couldn't say much then. I could not even repeat what my
brother and sister claim they told my father as he slipped
into his final coma. What good would it do? I laugh at her
last witticism, when I called her in the late spring from California: "So, Mother, is the snow gone yet?" "Oh yes. All
gone. Except on the ground of course." When I begin to fail,
you can simply let me go.

My Swedish grandfather set sail for America in the early

1900s. He raised seven children during the Depression and despite his old-world views on women, analogous to those he held on workers and unions, he put all six girls through college. For fifty years, his son and I share stories; we never once talk politics. For some sixty years, Granddad ate whatever my grandmother cooked for him, since it was not his place (he had no need to say directly) to interfere with what went on in the kitchen. At each meal, my grandmother served him canned peas. My mother tells me that as a child she once complained, only to be angrily hushed: "Dad likes them." That was that. Each meal of sixty years of family meals included the peas that Granddad required.

When my grandmother died in her eighties, my uncle, the one male in the family, took Granddad in and gave him his own room, which he had been surreptitiously constructing for years. When he later and laboriously raised the sink for the old man's convenience, poor Granddad could no longer use it as a urinal. He spoke for the first time in his life about these bodily functions, and my uncle restored the sink without complaint. My aunt of course served Granddad dinner, since he had never cooked for himself except perhaps on those fishing trips deep into the Rockies in the early twentieth century. In the photographs, you see him with his brothers lined up and the rows of fished-out trout before them. On the day my grandmother died, my aunt served him peas. He looked at them: "What is this?" "Canned peas, Dad. You always eat canned peas at dinner." "I've never liked them."

My aging mother is struggling to live alone. She calls me and announces she is moving to Bangor to be near my brother and sister. I ask why.

"Because that's what they want."

"Is that what you want?"

"It's what they want."

I put down the phone; I call my brother and later my sister: "Mother says she is moving to Bangor. Why is that?"

"Well, that's what she wants to do."

"Just for the record, what do you yourself want? Is it better to have her there? Or would you just as soon have her live alone in Brunswick?"

"Well, it's not really convenient to have her here, but it's what she wants."

I hang up. A second round of phone calls: "Mother, now Brother says that you're moving because that's what you want, even though it may not be what he wants. What is it you want?"

"Well, here in Brunswick, of course, would be . . ."

"Fine, you're staying there."

"Brother, now Mother says she's moving because that's what you want, even though it's not what she wants. What is it you want?"

"As I said, it's not really convenient . . ."

"Fine. She's staying in Brunswick."

"Sister, Mother . . ."

But why proceed with this?

I felt, of course, that I had finally introduced a new way

of speaking into the family. Rather than through loopy in-direction, four adults could speak the simple bos'n's truth to each other, even those taciturn, set-jaw, salty types like us. Mother must live independently; and yes, her driving was dangerous, but dangerous drivers are the price we pay for living in a free society. And yes, living with her during the summer was for me difficult; but we could learn the virtue of self-sacrifice from her own life, could we not?

Yet living alone, although convenient for us, was not easy for her. The bills got onerous and often were paid twice. Food was left on counters because she could not remember "where it went." When you or I forget "where things go," we just put them anywhere. For her, such things were paralyzing, and the bread went stale on the meticulously dusted tabletops. Finally, after years of such humiliation, she fell and broke her wrist in seven places. After weeks in the hospital, she moved from the coast where Father had sailed the boat she never once set foot in to the assisted living complex in Bangor near my brother and sister. It was, I was ashamed to think, a great relief to me.

I could tell the story of how she fell that October day, and how Linda Jane found her lying in the garage with her feet out the doorway in some hideous parody of the house-crushed witch in *The Wizard of Oz* and what she thought about during those eight hours in the autumn air and the two martinis and unreturned calls from her friends the next morning and the wrist swollen to twice its natural size, whatever nature is. I could tell all this, secondhand, from three different sources, but I have never been able to put the details together in a coherent way. It was decided. Mother moved to Bangor, despite all that I had done for her.

I don't know how many years then passed, maybe five, maybe more. By this time, she had died in a flurry of strokes. I was thinking of how she had suffered, the last few years of living alone, and the relief she felt after she moved to Bangor, even though she had sternly and quite publicly announced upon her arrival there that she would not associate with her fellow residents in the assisted-living complex. I suddenly realized what any intelligent person reading this knows already: when Mother moved to Bangor, we all got exactly what we wanted, even though we all claimed the reverse two years earlier. No one in my family has ever said anything directly, or expressed a simple desire, even when they knew what such a desire might be. And when I confronted my family individually so many years ago, no one reformed. The way one says, "I want X," has always been to say, "Mother wants X; Brother wants X." And because of my foolish attempts to change all this, Mother suffered for two or three meaningless and difficult years, stuck in the awful apartment building in winter with the contemptuous college students who knew nothing of the legends of her famous late husband.

As Mother got older, most of our conversations were of the past. The past we spoke of, however, was not one that she, growing up in the Rockies, had actually experienced. It was, rather, a past of a generation earlier, concerning what to her must have seemed a foreign coast. How did those quaint Victorians get to Maine in the painting from the 1870s with the cottage so alone and a nearly barren Lord's Point in the background? And she would tell me of the steamers she herself had never taken and how she had learned all this from "Mother Dane," so loathed by both of us. Why did she maintain, I wondered, this pretentious appellation, as if Mother Dane had produced kings and queens instead of a declining line of bourgeois academics and closet alcoholics? And why would she, immigrant's daughter that she was, repeat stories of this woman with the borrowed name who had put together that awful book of gencalogy with all the grim and bearded Victorians staring out of it and the male children posed in dresses? Why did the time that Mother Dane invented matter at all?

Today when these questions of Maine arise, I think I must ask Mother that. I think this even though I know that when I last raised such questions, all our conversations were conversations we had had before, when remnants of her intelligence and memories were focused on repeating back to me phrases she had used earlier, or phrases I myself had forgotten. Years after she stopped reading, she could analyze any book I gave her, simply by repeating back to me a version of my own critique of it. And this was well after her narrative faculties were all shot, along with the entire narrative of her life, and she could no longer understand irony or follow a baseball game on the radio or a routine drama on television. She became for me the language of myself reflected back to me. And still I ask of her these questions as I pose them, whose answers are distorted in the pretentious snobbery of Mother Dane.

THE FERRY DOCK AT MACKEREL COVE

I am on the wharf, next to the ferry dock at Mackerel Cove on Swan's Island. It is blowing thirty knots. I am holding on to the rail of my boat, which the wind has pinned immovably to the dock. It is like holding on to the same boat years earlier in the Kennebunk River at Chicks Marina.

In families such as mine, it can hardly be an accident that those most terrified of the water should choose to live on such an island, a twenty-five-minute ferry ride from Bass Harbor on a good day. The house owned by my sister faces east toward Great Duck Island and Frenchboro, and there the southeast wind from the water is the most persistent and the most violent. It is an irony but not, I think, an accident that when visiting I am whisked from the boat, as if it were a thing I hate, and walked along the land as the wind comes up and up, and finally to that house where the wind is most deafening. I finally insist on returning to the wharf and find my boat flattened to the wharf in the wind from the southwest.

My first attempt to extricate the boat fails: I steam forward a boat length, but the boat is driven by the wind hard right onto the perpendicular dock face and it is only my desperate reversal that keeps it from piling up on the ferry dock. Three of us inch the boat back along the wharf, around the corner so that it once more faces partially into the wind, that is, during the occasional settling moments of the wind. Suddenly, I am chastised by a family member. This really "won't do." My brother-in-law, I am informed, standing there calmly and silently, is actually terrified of the water. I must do better.

Why, I wonder, do I find myself standing on this dock, thinking of the first day years ago, when I stood on the dock in Kennebunk and felt the river current almost take the boat away from me? I vow I will never go ashore again on these trips, and at times I keep that vow. But of course, the gods laugh at the vows of lovers and embarrassed sailors.

In one of the sailing manuals, or perhaps in the words of someone repeating their banalities, it is said that mistakes are more quickly punished in sailing than in life. I did not fully believe that when I first heard it, and I don't believe it now. This is the self-laudatory thinking of those who have made more mistakes than they will admit, more perhaps than they have known or imagined: the rock under the keel near an unmarked anchorage in Western Bay Down East; the rocks surrounding my homeport of Harpswell, or the five-foot spot that becomes a four-foot spot on the lowest tides in Rockland, and which the boat bounces over, a terrible sensation. There are narrow misses about which I know nothing and I think I am a lucky and ignorant sailor. I have less fear as I grow older not because I have grown fearless or because I have less to fear, but because as I age, the chemicals of fear and anxiety that once coursed proudly through me have lessened in intensity.

So I am less upset, I suppose, thinking of Linda Jane in her domestic life twenty miles away from me in Los Angeles, not because I have come to terms with her behavior, not because I have matured into a greater understanding of what it is to love and be loved or of the transitory nature of life. I have simply outgrown the memories that once so tormented me.

Copland is now on my stereo, that most American of musics: the third section of *Rodeo*, or perhaps it is the second. I listen with unusual emotion. I am with Linda Jane, and we are watching the ABT or the Joffrey Ballet perform this from the cheap seats in the Dorothy Chandler Pavilion in Los Angeles. At the time, I had never heard this piece, something that now seems surprising to me, and I am overwhelmed with the movement—the movement of the dancers, the movement of the music, all of which she seems to know so well, even though she claims to despise such high-culture claptrap. And I wrote "Listening to Copland," on a bet from Linda Jane herself, about the bourgeois absurdities of golf. I am driving through Camden near Philadelphia. I am somewhere in New Orleans. With no thought of Linda Jane and no thought of sailing.

CHAPTER THIRTEEN

MOUNT DESERT AND SCHOODIC

Woke up at midnight. So bored I couldn't sleep.
—Commercial fisherman overheard
on Channel 68

It is perhaps my familial musings that keep me at this mooring in Northeast Harbor through the diminishing gale that finally seems sailable at 4 PM. I take my boat out through the compacted moorings and begin to hoist sail in the entrance. The night before, I coiled the main sheet differently from how I have coiled it for over twenty years. Beautiful and symmetrical, coiled as I had been recently advised, it now lies on the transom.

When the boat came into the wind, with the boom blown to the centerline, that beautiful coil would not come free. All my hand movements practiced for two decades would not untie it. I kept staring until the diminishing gale threw the boom against my temple. To this day I cannot recall whether the boat was in fact heading into the wind, as I have told the story here, or whether I was still steaming downwind through the harbor entrance. I cannot recall which way I myself was facing, forward or aft, when the boom hit me. I cannot recall whether the blood actually spattered on the floorboards as it did in the driveway to my Venice apartment as I was trying to get Linda Jane to the airport, or whether I am simply imagining that. I do recall the leisurely sail around the protected shores of Mount Desert as I considered blood and concussions and the un-manned boat sailing in circles, as Dick Nesbitt's boat is said to have done many years ago.

The anchorages here, as in an increasing number of Maine harbors, are filling up with moorings—rental moor-ings that cost what a motel room cost not long ago, private moorings largely unused by their owners, commercial moorings, and moorings that are no longer marked or used. There must be something one can do as the open water of Maine is privatized in this way: these open-water parking lots, like fish pens, like aquaculture of all sorts, like private floats and oversized docks, with their predictable "For Sale" signs as accessories. I pick up the town guest moorings off Spurling Cove, or in Cranberry Island, and think about my own dockless shore in Harpswell.

In Somes Sound, many sailors help themselves to an off-season mooring. You can also anchor in Valley Cove, be-neath the six-hundred-foot-high vertical wooded cliffs of St. Sauveur, although this takes some doing. The thrushes there sing in the evening light. The guidebooks rightly claim this is a glorious spot. But what I remember most is the bad way I played Maine one day, letting the chain links of the anchor rode rattle loudly on the deck as commercial fishermen might do.

I am sailing west, driven by the convenient east wind as the fog inevitably gives way to driving rain. Rather than sail against this to Northeast Harbor, I will continue through the Western Way of Mount Desert, across the bar off Bass Harbor Light, and eventually to the familiar harbor of Swan's Island. Due to the intricacy of these waters, you will not have the tide in your favor the entire way, whatever the conditions. You must sail against the tide either in the wide channel of the Western Way or across the bar at Bass Harbor Light. Standing so tall in the cockpit, I think my oilskins will keep the rain from the open hatchway. But that fails, and I spend three days sleeping in the water-soaked bunks.

Linda Jane drives me to the top of Cadillac Mountain. You can see far into the expanding water surface, and it reminds me of looking down into the fog from the top of the mountain decades earlier, when I was stranded with Charlie and Nancy and Linda Jane on their spacious and beautiful *Sceptre,* Alberg-designed like all my boats would be, in Northeast Harbor, the fog too dense to sail in. Linda Jane rows me around the harbor. She has driven here. Tomorrow, we will step expertly from the boat as it glides past the dock and she will drive me home. It is like driving home at sixteen from Mount Desert with Linda Jane—a real adventure, that, forced onto the shoulder in the hailstones!—or twenty years later on a quiet July evening, back from the opera house at Somesville. Linda Jane wades into the icy water to her waist, hours before curtain time in Somesville. I have been listening to Beethoven, which John, now dead, then plays for us. I think of the long ride home. We step onto the dock, knowing we will never sail together again and hardly sailed on this trip. I can tell by the way she glances at the buildings on the banks of Northeast Harbor that she is not fully with me and never has been fully with me and will never be so again. We say nothing, as she rows as her patient father taught her, past the fog-softened cottages of Northeast Harbor.

THE FOG AT WINTER HARBOR

Winter Harbor is the last usable harbor before rounding Schoodic Point to what for the sailor is truly Down East: Prospect Harbor, the tiny bowl of Corea (a bad place to be becalmed, even on a good day), and the bar at Petit Manan. Sand Cove, the most westerly and open of the three coves that form Winter Harbor, has a yacht club with a shockingly well-constructed clubhouse, a beautiful fleet of old, wooden racing sloops, and a well-kept golf course on the northwest corner. On all but the most blustery of evenings you can watch the golfers walk their slow routes down the fairways, pursuing their curious sport where even the best shot is a penalty. Sand Cove, with its deep water and numbered moorings, thus seems the least authentic place on this authentic coast. I stop at the clubhouse. They will not have ice or an attendant until July.

By the time I spent two days in Winter Harbor, waiting in the fog and windlessness, Linda Jane had left me for the last time. She had become Linda Jane, and I wasted time in the cabin, thinking of such things as acceptance. *Forsan et haec olim meminisse juvabit,* I thought sophomorically: better to talk about that week of fog or those three days sleeping in the sailbag in this same boat years ago, waiting for the gale to break. Better to recall the inadequate love than to reexperience it.

You do not expect liveaboards this time of year in these waters, but there is one next to me, anchored in the deep water of Sand Cove. He works, I think, running tour boats through the fog past the Porcupines to Bar Harbor and back, and I am flattered that even he, relying on a radar screen and GPS, complains about the fog and vows never to take this job again. In late morning, he will pass me in the fog as I sail toward what will soon be the distinctive shape of Schoodic Point. Under power, he will wave, with a trace of deference, but he will not know I am only playing Maine in my elaborate calculations of the rhumb line as I tack south through the bay; I expect the fog to clear and I will have the easiest of sails Down East.

Still shy of Schoodic Point, I encounter what I call the circle of fog, although I've never seen it so described. Visibility can be judged, not by the density of fog, which cannot really be perceived, but by the shape of what is visible. As long as there are irregularities, whether overhead, or toward a shore, or deep along the surface of the water, you can call this "patchy" fog, and what is known as "visibility" will be acceptable. But there is a moment, sailing in the fog, where the fog closes to a perfect circle, marking the limits of sight on the water. At times, this becomes a dome, with the time of day lost overhead. The circle tightens and becomes more regular and perfect and as its perfection and tautness grows, all is lost but the compass and the compass rose on the chart.

And I am writing this in that circle, or, rather, as the circle breaks and the irregularities of land, of buoys, of memories of lives lived by loved ones, break that circle and at times even break through with what is called a scale-up, leading to what might be also known as, say, the "sparkling clarity of a sailing day in Maine." It is easy to be accepting of things at such times: either in that dome of fog, far from a mark you need to make, or just when those irregularities appear and all is going right. When you are well paid, and your work is read, your lover smiles, or when the boat glides along at three to five knots in smooth water. Acceptance is then an easy thing.

Linda Jane's infidelities were always simple and predictable, I imagine in that dome of fog. They were things one could revel in, like the distant, unthreatening thunder or the calm. She visits her once lover in the unknown regions of New York; she takes up with her husband; she stares across the water to things you cannot see. You could feel and you could rage, you think, and the imagined pain made life and its purposes clear. But most faithlessness is not like that at all, I think, still sailing in the fog. It is one's own, not that of Linda Jane.

Is it not a perversity of human psychology that one's greatest erotic memories are catastrophes? And is this too like the memories of my sailing days? Why are the disasters and the errors so fixed in the memory? Why are the good days lost in the bad clichés used to describe them? Where, I think, are the rushes of emotion I must have felt with Linda Jane? Why are those wasted on bad lovers and not the real passion of life—Linda Jane, whose voice and touch I can barely recall today? Did she stroke me? or was that some ample hipped hippie girl in Portsmouth? Did she stare at me? or was that the French-speaking surrogate whose passion even then I dismissed as professional? Did she hold me? smile or laugh at me? What were the once-momentous things she said? There seems, I grandly think, not a trace of all that left.

I waste my memories instead on those who never mattered or mattered only briefly. On the women whose bodies were all wrong or mine all wrong and the women I couldn't talk to. Those lovely distant girls of twenty, or thirty, or distant girls of forty. The once teenagers now grown into obesity and depression and drug addiction.

I have left a log of sailing days and know the winds of each day I have sailed Down East, but I have nothing of the sort for my life with Linda Jane, fearing that there might be some unpleasant truth there. Linda Jane, who came to adulthood in the '70s (such a different time!), once said she could not remember whether she had slept with a roommate. I claimed then that that was impossible. And I thought at that moment of another Linda Jane, who came to adulthood in the '80s, who claimed to have had a different lover for each day of the year, and that too was impossible. And I answered I don't need a logbook to remember each of them and at times the smell of them and the things they said or I thought they said and the way they kissed or pretended to. The sailing days may blur together, but these, I remember insisting at the time, do not.

And I thought then, lying back and laughing at Linda Jane, that all these retorts were ridiculous, since there was nothing better than a lover who couldn't remember who it was she had slept with. And I lay there that night recounting not the lovers, but the days on the water. I remembered then with absolute clarity sailing to Isle au Haut, heading toward the western anchorage at Moore's Harbor, but catching the breeze and turning north toward another thoroughfare, these memories now intermingled with a dream of sailing through the dredged passage between the main island of Isle au Haut and Kimball Island. And I knew then the conditions and the depths at Pickering Cove in Deer Isle and even the thunderstorm I endured there and what anchor I threw overboard in the rain.

I claimed I did not understand this wanting not to know.

What is to be forgotten, I said then, is something else: one's misdeeds and juvenile and adult stupidities, the banalities of adults unable to deal with you. The idiocies of what once passed for wit. The abstruse taxonomies of the good.

Forgetting, she claimed, or I did as the discussion wore on long into the evening, was a form of acceptance, was it not? No different, she said, from the embracing of a memory—that long log of lovers one never desecrates by consulting. But the task, here in the fog, is to forget this, she said, or forget a part of it; the task here is to reconstitute all this in a time when there are no missed rendezvous; and no failing provisions and ice worn out and water all gone stale. No lack of novels or novelties or chords to play whenever one's hands grow callous. And no broken thermoses and vegetables gone bad and wet clothes and, say, the Red Sox on a West Coast swing when the games start when you're asleep. One's husband on the West Coast, she must have thought, forgetting even this.

She sleeps and, once again, shy of Down East, I am lost with Linda Jane. And it is remarkable, I think, I can speak of loss this way. As if, say, as here, it is nothing more than being in the fog or, say, misplacing one of your dozen pairs of reading glasses, or a lock wrench, or the camera, or, ashore, a tie, the cell phone, or your car keys.

On a boat, there are procedures to ensure that neither this supreme nor these minimal states of loss occur. In a boat's very limited space, each object has its place, and it hardly matters what the logic of locations is, since the mind can accommodate, say, a hundred objects without plan or order, but only with difficulty the logic of a rational ordering of even a few of them.

So I think, dreaming next to Linda Jane, that on my boat I have never lost my tools or my food or flashlights, or even my writing paper or pens and gum erasers or navigational dividers or winch handles or tiny bits of lines with their precisely assigned functions. I have lost none of these things—no guide or chart with its compass rose, where the way is always clearly indicated. And if I broke such objects, or misplaced them in the rain, or dropped them overboard, sitting, say, on my reading glasses, I have never lost their spares, which are in the single but half-jammed drawer beneath the sink.

She sleeps, and I recount the things I forgot on this trip: battery-powered fly swatter (a joke gift but surprisingly useful), gloves, tweezers, Duck tape (or is it duct tape?), white tape, and decaf coffee; anemometer, chopping knife, paper towels, new fishing line, a loaf of bread, butter, books, 9-volt lantern and battery; staple gun for the Velcro of the mosquito net, rice noodles, plates, hand soap, hat, short-handled screwdriver, crew, herbal tea, foghorn (home in the plastic wrap), stove alcohol (to look for the can I had bought the day I left would be to admit forgetting bringing it aboard), light bulbs for cabin light.

Things I took too much of, so I think, as she sleeps so beautifully: my third tube of toothpaste, broken saltines, clothes, hat, loaf of bread, cabbage, plates, paper and clip-board, art supplies from five years ago; cheese, cream, an-chors, a chess set from ten years ago when I tried to supplement one summer the chess-tactics book I read on a fourteen-hour trip to Wales to see Linda Jane.

The train left Birmingham at 9 PM in the rain.

Note that some items appear on both these lists.

PART V

DOWN EAST
AND BEYOND
DOWN EAST

CHAPTER FOURTEEN

DOWN EAST

He don't need to go lobsterin'.
—Tom Coffin

For a long time, I woke up early here. In the morning fog, islands disappear, hiding some of the devastation wrought on them—the summer homes bloated with the water and septic systems blasted into a once-unspoiled island. These are blemishes of those who play Maine in what I'll call "the wrong way," so I imagine sailing here. No one retires to an island or an oceanside cottage in, say, Milbridge, just as no one retires to those giant shingled fortresses I have by-passed on Isleboro in Penobscot Bay. These are places you can invite friends to for the weekend and talk about painting, or poetry, or property, or whatever the obscenely rich discuss, as the weight of things like human waste sinks deeper into the broken rock you claim to love.

I am sailing Down East at last, but I cannot rid myself of the images I came here to escape. I understand people must live in Maine and will build houses in Maine, and remake Maine landscape into their images of the way Maine landscape ought to be. But at some point, law and good sense should inform us that we don't need to clear-cut a path to the water, and even maintain the one that has been there for decades, and that the basic requirement for houses and docks should not be simply "larger than the one next to it." There are in fact new houses on the coast with color and shape that reproduce the color and shape of what is or once was there and I should acknowledge them. A Harpswell house facing east across the sound, still set perfectly into the landscape despite the devastation of the Patriots' Day storm; the house on Grog Island in the Deer Island Thorofare off Stonington.

I can accept such structures as a matter of tradition, or defining tradition in that strange and unnatural way we define the tradition of boat design or boat operation itself. I know the grand shingled cottages in Prouts Neck and Kennebunk were once as much a blight on the landscape as anything one defines as less tasteful there today. Those shingled classics with their servant quarters in a coast already clear-cut for sheep, building material, and firewood. It was to these once-revolting homes, I suppose, my relatives steamed for their Maine vacations and learned the accent and loved the beach roses and sailed and, like my uncle Joe, dressed in ridiculous bathing suits and walked out to the water on the cobblestone beach with an even then old-fashioned thermometer set into a block of wood with a lanyard, and refused to swim until it read 70 degrees, which it rarely if ever did. That must have been itself traditional in

those days, since Roger Angell tells the same anecdote of
E. B. White, and he certainly did not get it from me.

I feel a nostalgia for this time not because it was better
than our time, which it was not, but because I was young on
that stone beach, and the cottages that had already torn
that landscape smelled of the water and the beach mold and
roses, and the time they represented had always, so it
seemed, been exactly as times were then. To find such a
stone beach now, you have to drive past the shingled cottages reaching all the way to Milbridge, on to Campobello.
I walked on such cobblestones with the sea moss drying in
the sun, and that was before I experienced anything I knew
as change. There were no insulting playmates on that shore
or belligerent neighbors and fishermen and landowners en-
forcing their supposed riparian rights, and there were wonderfully negligent parents as there would not be today, and
life was as it could have been forever, so it seemed, like that
of those men my father had played with, those gay and
preppy teenagers who grew into my uncles and led their ec-
centric lives there until their businesses failed and they shot
themselves, leaving all they owned to their sisters. These
men were there with their secrets and thought maybe I
would grow into the culture they established there. But I
did not grow into it, a blessing of the hatred I felt for the
bourgeois complacencies of my grandmother, who, with
those gay and narrow uncles, ruined collectively the peace
of my father and made life possible.

Down East is the end of this trip or the goal of it, and thus there seems little difference here bound east or west. There are tides and fog and extremes of cold which all the guidebooks note, and few places to stop, but everyone who reads the sailing guides knows all that.

The first time I sailed to Roque Island, I sailed around it in the afternoon, screaming as I sailed, and as I sailed back through the channel into the sheltered bay, I continued to shriek in ebullience with every tack. It was Sunday, and working fishermen go there for picnics, I suppose, anchoring off the beach near the half-exposed fish weir before running home in the evening. The captain of the *Silver Dollar* circled me at anchor on his way home, and as his wife warned needlessly of the anchor rode, he said I sure looked like I was having fun, and characterized my position in the cove as "Just about perfect," as it has never quite been since.

By the time I got here, even that first time, it was pointless to pretend to be an explorer, and now when I arrive I think of little beyond the problems involved in sailing home against the prevailing winds. Given diesel power and GPS and radar and chartplotters, none of what the sailing guides say in abject flattery of their readers who get to this still-awful (I'll say) place is true, since anyone who can play with charts and a joystick can navigate to Roque Island or any other place on the coast of Maine, just as I have done following different but equally arbitrary conventions and traditions.

So now, there are simply things there that I wish to see,

and there is little left there I need to experience. The islands just visible in a tantalizing morning fog. The desolate flatness of the water. The wake of the boat in a convenient tide. The puffins and the auks, which I associate for some reason with my brother. Did he point these out to me in the Peterson birdbook? Had he seen one on some exotic bird-watching trip that I was too young to participate in? And how could my memories of Down East cross with those of him? our adult lives now diverse, and our childhoods filled with sports and baseball statistics?

It is always, somehow, Petit Manan, and I am always bound east at slack tide past Petit Manan Light toward Trafton Island or west in the outgoing tide in the late morning, through the bar or outside past the light again. All this seemed once a miracle to me, but you can do this easily even in the densest fog. There are only two marks you need to make. The guidebooks proudly claim you will be tidebound or fog-bound here, but for me, the days Down East become for the first time calculable: a return west to Winter Harbor and Mount Desert. To Deer Isle and Vinalhaven. And finally, the halfday sail to Rockland, where Linda Jane inevitably waits with her exquisite provisionings.

LETTERS FROM VIETNAM

James lives in Cutler, although he lists his home as East Machias. He is visiting me on his way to New York, and from New York he will eventually end, he says (or denies), in Vietnam. From New York, he will fly to San Francisco.

From San Francisco, he will fly west. Years later, he will tell me he was never certain where he landed next. On the way west, he was told he was in Guam. On the way east, he was told he was in Hawaii. But it was the same airfield. Between these two landings, he served with the adjutant general in Vietnam, a famously cushy and nonviolent assignment, or so I, stateside, was assured. He was trained as a translator. He weighed 280 pounds.

James was the first person I knew who was intelligent enough to keep two contradictory ideas in his head at the same time. When he visited me on the way to Vietnam, he ate voraciously, and talked incessantly about getting his weight to 300 pounds. At 300 pounds, he would be too heavy to serve in Vietnam. Or so he said. He had it all figured out. Cased. I don't know whether this policy on weight was true or simply part of military apocrypha. Nonetheless, he was on his way to Vietnam, all 280-plus pounds of him, and he had made no plans to do anything else. Since I had not yet experienced this same behavior in people like Linda Jane and in so many of my academic colleagues, I was confused, thinking simply: you either go to Vietnam, or you do not go to Vietnam. You step on the scale, and you either weigh over 300 pounds, or you do not. You cannot, I thought naively, do both or weigh both simultaneously.

He wrote long letters. I wrote back. It was a somewhat snarled conversation, in which each response was to statements made in at least two letters in the past. Later, I realized that James never really listened to the response. He simply ranted, and to readers as young as I was, it gave the illusion of intimacy.

He had a lover. She was a prostitute. But their relationship, he claimed, was different from relationships she had with all other men. He, and he alone, did not pay for her affections. Instead, he kept her in an apartment in Saigon and paid all her expenses, even, if I remember correctly and if what he told me was true to begin with, the expenses of her young child. He believed they were in love. And I assume this is the same belief anyone who hires a prostitute must indulge in. That, of course, is what you pay for. The physical aspects you can get on your own.

Three years later James is running a local road race in Machias. He hasn't trained, and in those days, before we learned that even the most ordinary of middle-aged men and women can run marathons, the 10k distance seemed immense. When we were in high school, it was thought that one should take tablets when exercising to replace the loss of salt. I can see the white salt tablets in the coaches' hands. It all seemed so mysterious; I couldn't understand the complexities of chemical regulations of unknown body fluids, and fortunately, I wouldn't touch them. Twenty years later we were told this was counterproductive and that we should not take salt but drink water instead. Several years after that, I almost passed out having drunk nearly two gallons of water during a marathon; we were told then (too late) that dehydration was less dangerous than overhydration. Perhaps I should have taken the salt tablets in the first place. Perhaps I should have realized that growing older sometimes makes you even more naive and impressionable than staying young.

James had no access to all this contradictory information, and wouldn't have been bothered by its contradictions if he had. So he took his salt tablets, relying on the wisdom of the myths we learned in high school, which never changed. Predictably, he did all this in excess, swallowing not one but a handful. He died halfway through the race, somewhere around a pitiful mile four.

The letters James wrote were his own sailing narrative, both as he constructed it and as I read and responded to it so belatedly. He is of course involved in both the beginning and the end, for it was James whom I was visiting from Portsmouth in my opening chapter here.

> I'm a driver [he writes], and I'm driving my lieutenant
> through Saigon, and he gets out and the engine is
> running and I turn it off and I'm standing around be-
> side the jeep and he is talking to someone I am hear-
> ing music like rock music somewhere and I am
> standing beside the jeep on one side or the other
> when he comes back. The routine is I am supposed to
> open the door to the jeep for the lieutenant but I am
> spaced out and open the door to the driver's side
> where I am standing and he needs to sit on the other
> side and he says "That's the wrong door, soldier!" and
> instead of snapping to attention and saying "Yes sir!"
> I walk to the other side and pretend to be stupid and
> say "Ah yes, that's the difference between officers and

enlisted men" no wait, that's not it that's not what he said, I was standing there, and he says "you need to put the key in the ignition to start it, soldier!" and that's when I said "Ah, that's the difference between officers and grunts," meaning you're so much smarter than me, and he's all pissed off and starts shouting and I'm thinking about what Heidegger said or at least what Prof. X used to say about Heidegger you know he would take that deep breath "Gentlemen!" he would say . . .

The letters would go on for pages. And I would respond, "I am sitting here typing and Linda Jane is gone to ride horses somewhere and I'm reading Sartre and writing this novel and Sartre says . . ." These exchanges continued for months, I think, and it was the pages of these exchanges that James would read when I visited him for the last time in Cutler. He did not read the letters I had written but his own, which he had carefully retrieved somehow, I don't remember how, from me and from his other correspondents. He would lie in bed, smoking, stoned, reading page after page after page of what he had written from Vietnam, and all this was to come together some day as a fictional romance or New Journalism rant of some kind. Meanwhile, he had time to read my own novel, which is now in a box somewhere, and imagine who should play the surrealistic characters in the movie, then go back to those long long letters on their yellow legal pads.

There were always several points of time involved in these reading sessions: James on his bed reading, and

James writing that letter (where? in bed next to his prostitutes?), and whatever was the ostensible subject of that letter. These three points of time then coalesced for him in such a drug-filled haze that it finally made no sense to him and could not have made sense to anyone else. At some point in the afternoon as I was retyping my manuscript, he would get up and say that we should go for a walk in the alien landscape of Down East Maine. There is deep moss underfoot and moss like Spanish moss in the tree heights—Usnea, I'm told it is—and it reminds me now as it could not then of my time in a much distant New Orleans. The most vivid memory I have of these walks is the hour we spent with a partridge perched high above us, on a branch or maybe exposed in silhouette on a power line. One of us, it must have been James, tossed a piece of muck up there to flush it. We wanted to see it fly. It was impervious. The mud became a dirt clod. Nothing. The dirt clods became small stones. One passed within an inch of the partridge's head, and it moved not in the slightest. This sent us both into fits of laughter. More rocks, now thrown with force. James finally brought the bird down. We stripped off its feathers and must have cooked it somehow, but all I remember is the bird's placid stare, slightly to the right, as the first rock passed within inches of it.

In the interchangeable bays I sail to, my moments on the water become indistinguishable from all other moments on the water; they are reduced to a set of points and incidents that barely show any continuity at all. You would think, would you not, that sailing is about movement and slow but perceptible progressions, where one has time to experience all the details of the seascape. Nothing happens quickly, and often the passage through the water is more consistently smooth and controlled than any passage elsewhere might be. It is, in essence, or it could be, the very embodiment of continuities: the continuity of wind and water, where the boat effectively flies through the air, buoyed on the water, where air and sea are the same and the mist in the air is the mist of the sea and the foam in the sea is the mixing of the wind and the sea. But the memory works in exactly contrary fashion, conditioned as it is by the shoeboxes of snapshots and photographs that form these memories for me.

Fat James weighs 300 pounds and I doubt at his funeral that anyone ever read his eulogy. He ended, I hear, abandoning the Vietnam novel or memoir or whatever it might have been and tearing down an old building in hopes of building his own cabin. I, oddly, did the same thing: ripping up old porches one summer and building a small and now-embarrassing ramshackle cabin in the woods where I could work undisturbed on my unpublished novels and on my dissertation, entitled "Words and Things . . ." like an earlier section here. James never got to the building stage, because his cabin would have to be a far better one than mine, and that precluded the building of it. I hear, I think, that he took up with some woman and child in Machias, who must have been versions of his beloved prostitute and child in Vietnam and they spent a few months wasted on whatever drugs were popular up there at the time. The letters stopped, because their banalities were finally unendurable, even to me, and he wandered aimless through the foreign cultures of Machias looking for whatever it was he had briefly seen in those crazed and formless letters he had constructed in the alienating cities of Asia.

CHAPTER FIFTEEN

GETTING GAY

Winch jammed. Took two weeks of slack from the foot rope.
—Trawler captain overheard on Channel 68

The phrase David used when we were fishing was "getting gay." It had none of its now-popular associations then, but those are what gives it all its force today. The phrase "getting gay" was always an admonition; maybe I would move "a little too smartly" leaping into the skiff or handling a trap, with its complexities of lines: "Don't get too gay out there [and start capering about]." Or: "He got a little gay and [fell overboard. And Wes couldn't swim, like a lot of fishermen can't, but I always said, Jesus Christ, Wes . . .]." The most dangerous time on any boat is paradoxically when everything goes right, because that is when, unthinking, you tend to "get a little gay." In life, this may work differently. Perhaps you don't do anything; perhaps you just go on. You remember later how grand it all was. You reconstruct it in your memory, inventing extravagant detail. In boats, when things go right, "too right," the admonitions say, the temptation to "get gay" simply overwhelms you.

You act as if invincible. You one-hand seventy-pound lobster traps (or maybe they were forty pounds) from starboard to port and ruin your back for decades; you race to the bow with no hands, or let the boat heel until the rail goes under and the water laps into the cockpit.

When I first sailed to Roque Island, I decided to take the inside passage back, through Jonesport and under the bridge, which in my boat can be negotiated only at low tide. I dieseled out in the morning, clearing the Jonesport Bridge either by five feet or by five inches. I raised sail, or part of it, and roared, I thought, through Tibbett Narrows in the southwest wind, "a real smoky sou'wester," it would be said, Grandfather gaily adding "A-yuh," and roared inside "the Ladle" to investigate Cape Split Harbor and, since it was barely noon, roared back out of the harbor into Eastern Bay. The next day would provide the perfect northwest wind, so Art Lester assured me on NOAA radio, to carry me out past Petit Manan and back to Winter Harbor. And, having never sailed this route, I of course had it planned perfectly. There is really, I thought, nothing to all this.

I would be well dug in, I thought, even using the precise expression for securely anchoring, before the squalls marking the wind shift, southwest to northwest, tracked through the harbor. I gaily sailed in Eastern Bay, around Shipstern Island and out past the Pot and the Ladle, islands seldom so visible in the Down East haze, then gaily back into Cape Split Harbor as the haze grew dense, this time with the jib stowed and the CQR anchor on the bow. I had picked my spot on the first run through. I roared sailing downwind past the Southwest Harbor harbormaster, it turned out, who was securely moored on the public moorings, and let the whole business go, that is, the CQR (so perfect for these conditions) and the perfectly calculated length of anchor rode and chain. I was sailing downwind at what is called full throttle, and I must have been an impressive sight even in those hard-bitten waters.

That is what getting gay is all about.

The boat sailed to the end of its tether like the bulldog chasing the cat in old cartoons, then, as the anchor caught, the boat snapped smartly 180 degrees just (as I thought) like in the movies, although this of course is just as smartly never done in the movies. And with supreme confidence and competence, and as gaily as possible, I dropped sail and started to pretend to attend to the things that needed attending, as if this were a routine I had followed dozens of times in the past few weeks. It was only then, with the sails down, that I noticed, or began to realize I was noticing, after a self-congratulatory pause, that the rock bank downwind on the north shore of Otter Cove (the sole acceptable anchoring spot in the harbor)—that rock bank was getting closer.

I had been on badly anchored boats before, so I knew or thought I knew exactly what to do. I turned on the engine, cursed as if silently, but loud enough for the Southwest Harbor harbormaster to hear, and slowly slowly began to retrieve the dragging anchor. Slowly. And the boat itself finally circled slowly, according to an intricate formula whose name I have forgotten now, around its focal point, the steadily slipping anchor.

Anchors are generally identified by weight. There are times you "need" a heavier anchor, so you are told, since, say, a twenty-pound anchor, but not a ten-pound one, will "pierce," as they say, the obstinately thick layer of kelp that lines the bottom of some harbors in Down East Maine. There is just enough reason in all this to convince you it is true. But the very premise is nonsense, and it is hardly possible in the short space of a chapter to prove the errors involved in such thinking. The words themselves are inapplicable. How could anyone forget that although the specific gravity of galvanized steel is high, it is not up there with lead and plutonium, and thus what on my boat is a "heavy" twenty-pound anchor weighs much less than that in the water, particularly, so I read, in water approaching its maximum density achieved at 39 degrees Fahrenheit? And does one imagine that a twenty-pound anchor, "heavy" on a small boat, will penetrate that kelp to the firm mud beneath, but "undersized" on a larger boat, will somehow slip helplessly across the weed?

An anchor's weight, in and of itself, is irrelevant, either for piercing kelp or for holding a boat generally. A large anchor buries more surface area in the mud and it will not break as easily as a smaller one. That's all there is to it. And if you believe in the kelp-piercing qualities of weight alone,

why, you can easily enough conduct an experiment, by dragging a dozen or so various-sized CQRs over some kelp you
might pick up, cut, say, from your neighbor's mooring and
strewn across the soft-turned earth of your spring garden.

Until you raise the anchor and examine it, it is difficult
to know what that anchor has done on the bottom, and impossible to know how it has obtained its variant efficien-
cies. All that weed piercing and seeking of the firm black
mud famous in Maine harbors, the resetting in the wind
shift—on an anchored boat, all that is pure speculation.

So here, in Cape Split Harbor, my particular anchor,
however well chosen for Down East harbors, had found
none of that secure black mud said to lie beneath the kelp
there, and instead, bearing far more weight than it had
taken to the bottom, came slowly slowly to the surface as
my wake formed its now-incalculable curves in the harbor.

When it (whatever "it" is) finally broke the surface, I was
steaming (as they say) in ignominious and remarkably un-
gay circles to the watchful eye of the Southwest Harbor harbormaster. What I circled, now ignoring him as best I could
instead of cursing for his enjoyment, seemed a small island
of sorts—a brown dome of kelp and weeds and mud and
somewhere within all that an anchor. Circling now un-gaily,
I cut as much of this debris free as I could, because in a pre-
ceding paragraph, you have learned that the weight of an
object in air is significantly more than the weight of the
same object in water, particularly objects with low specific

gravities, like wet kelp and soft mud, and as soon as the island of debris broke the surface of the water into the liberating air, it was unmanageable.

After another round or two of cutting, I found that beneath the cut-away kelp was a bag of what I believe were mussels or oysters. I remember them as oysters, but I do not know why I remember them that way. Did it weigh one hundred pounds? Were there really that many hundreds of dollars abandoned? I cannot remember whether I actually got this aboard, but I doubt I could have done that. So I will say instead that I cut and finally dumped the oysters or clams or mussels and kelp, or at least cut them free from my anchor flukes and stowed the anchor and steamed sheepishly to the unused mooring next to the harbormaster. Years later, I found him again, this time on the Manset dock in Southwest Harbor. He pretended to recognize me, but what he recognized was likely only my unchanged boat. "Didn't I once see you . . ." he began. I pretend to find the whole incident merely amusing. He graciously pretended he did so too.

In circumstances such as that, beheld by those who can both deride you and help you, getting gay will likely lead to no more than ignominy. Under a watchful audience, on a noncommercial boat, there is little need for concern. But there are other moments when this is not the case. There are instruments aboard to navigate in fog. Mine have no chartplotting screens or visuals. They have merely numbers, and I delude myself into believing that these numbers, abstract as they are, get me closer somehow to the realities of navigation than would the large color chartplotting screens you will find in other boats or the maps and icons on the TomTom of the average car.

Among the important sets of numbers are those labeled BRG, or "bearing," that is, the direction you need to go to a particular target, and COG, or "course over ground," that is, the direction in which you are actually traveling. Ideally, you want these two figures to be the same. And if they are not the same (and they usually are not the same), it is a bad time to get gay; you may well end up in the predicament described by Garrison Keillor and experienced by all winter drivers—staring out the window on a dark snowy evening, trying to follow the tire track in the snow only to realize the tire track you are following has been put there by your left front tire.

When you confuse BRG with COG, at first the two readings diverge. If you are thinking clearly, you will stop and consider this divergence. If you get gay, you will steer slightly to the right. The two readings diverge more. Since all is otherwise going well, you then assume your correction was inadequate as most corrections are and you steer farther to the right. They diverge even more. If things have been going extremely well in the fog (which is what caused you to get a little gay in the first place), you begin to think serenely about the nature of Down East tides, about compass error, about the inevitable distortions of fog, about the peculiarities of perception, all the while steering resolutely to the right and always watching the numbers diverge. It's like sailing against a tide, you laugh: if you sail badly enough, the tide will always end up in your favor. BRG and COG will always finally be the same, like real time and the time indicated on the stopped clock, or even on the clock running hours fast. Sailing serenely in fog is always a case of getting gay. I was broken from this reverie by the wrong but well-marked buoy passing ominously to my left.

MASKING AT MARDI GRAS

It is Mardi Gras in New Orleans, a long way from sailing conditions. You could buy old Krewe costumes for a dollar or two anywhere; so I bought from the nearest secondhand store a faux courtier jacket that Linda Jane enhanced by staying up all night sewing for herself its more or less Pre-Raphaelite counterpart. We are both a "long way from home," and it will be a point of pride years later, sailing Down East, to be told the same thing, thanks to the words "South Harpswell" now largely inscribed on the stern. In New Orleans, the difference between locals and those "from away" is simpler on Mardi Gras than it is in Maine. The locals include anyone who lives there and does not just come for the holiday, and on this day, even I thus qualify. We locals here ignore the partying associated with Mardi Gras on the days leading up to it. Such things merely get in the way of daily life. But we "mask" for the day itself, that is, get ourselves done up in ridiculous costumes, when those "from away" are too tired to participate much, or are content to watch, or are already on their way to the airport.

Professor Longhair used to play on Tchoupitoulas or was it Magazine Street, and I worked nights in the Medical Records Department of the hospital. Everyone who held that job was a poet or novelist or party girl or just a dead beat doing her nails and letting the hysterical calls for medical records pile up while the patients in the emergency room died because no one knew what they were allergic to. My coworker was a party girl and maybe a poet as well and thus needed to see Professor Longhair even though she had signed up to work the Monday night before Fat Tuesday, the day itself. I took half her shift only on the absolute promise she made and incredibly kept to show up at 2 AM I think it was so I could go home and get a half night's sleep before Mardi Gras. I rode home on my bicycle and in my costume thinking of the beautiful but cold Linda Jane and I had been in bed no more than ten minutes when I heard the confusion of my friend Joe from Baton Rouge trying to get in the door and upstairs.

I never got the story straight. I think he was just being gay and crying and lost and the cabbie threw him out in the middle of Jena Street in front of the two stone dogs that guarded the stairs to my apartment. Then he crawled whining and weepy up the stairs between the stone dogs and made no more sense than they did.

When Joe drank, he also got amorous. My $60/month

apartment had so many bedrooms I used to move just for the novelty of it or to say that I had done so, but there was no explaining this to him on that night. And when it was clear that amorous Joe would not sleep or act other than amorous Joe, I simply got up and left him whining in bed and put on coffee and put my costume back on, with its wine-flask accessory, and biked across the city ruined decades later by Katrina at dawn to my beautiful but steely cold Linda Jane. I hadn't drunk in years and hardly tasted wine in my life. We rode the bus downtown and got there by 7 AM was it? Pete Fountain's Half-Fast Walking Club was already finished for the day. There was a chicken carcass in the street and I lectured to it. A week earlier, three of us had been riding our bikes on Gentilly Avenue for some reason, and for some other reason reciting Shakespeare, working out the familiar speeches—Mercutio's death speech, for example—and after a dozen blocks, I had most of it. And now, a week later, drunk and sleepless with my beautiful Linda Jane on my arm in her faux Pre-Raphaelite costume in New Orleans on Mardi Gras, the first person I saw shouted serendipitously, "Mercutio! Mercutio!" and I turned, and gave her a drunken version of the complete death-speech. Or maybe just more of it than you could get on Canal Street that morning.

Then it is October, past sailing season, and I am on a Western Airlines plane from Los Angeles headed to the Midwest. I realize the seat I am in could be that of the husband of Linda Jane, who is waiting for me in Nebraska. When she greets me at the airport, there is another small group waiting for arriving passengers, and she insists that we witness the small drama they have concocted. One of them, Linda Jane explains, has never met what airlines call "the Arriving Passenger." This stranger is scripted to run up to the Arriving Passenger as soon as he emerges; she will throw her arms around him and say how wonderful it is to see him while the two friends watch and collapse in laughter, or so they have scripted it. And we will watch.

Does Linda Jane expect this to be amusing? It isn't really, because the Arriving Passenger only smiles in partial amazement, knowing instantly he is the object of some joke he doesn't fully understand. It is not interesting. It is entirely predictable. And Linda Jane grows sullen, perhaps realizing at that moment that there is not much difference between these two or three unwitting play-actors and ourselves.

We walk to the parking lot. I drive her car back through the now-familiar but then still-alien night landscape of Midwest America. In three days, I will be driving this same route in the early morning to catch my Western Airlines plane back to Los Angeles, and in six months, it will be nearly sailing season once again.

CHAPTER SIXTEEN

BOUND WEST

Well there. It was so . . . so . . . well there.

—D. Pulsifer

ART LESTER

Art Lester died today. He was swimming in Sebago Lake near his small sailboat, which had broken free from its mooring. I understand he was swimming from his boat or from the mooring toward the shore. When you are our age, and you swim out to do something easy—adjust a line, tie a knot—you will be surprised at how difficult it is to work unsupported in the water. Cutting the seaweed from my own mooring that same summer, I swam back to shore exhausted, my arms scratched by the growth on the unused pennant. Art Lester did not make it back to shore. I imagine he was trying to board his boat, and found that, at our age, that is impossible. So he swam to shore, and he swam too late to shore. He had an alternative: but clinging helplessly to his own boat while the neighbors called for help, that was an undignified way to go.

Art Lester's is a voice I know very well. Until 1997, he announced the weather on the National Weather Service radio. There is not a day I ever sailed before 1997 when I did not hear him. He was replaced by a computer, called Paul, but whom we all called Sven because of his weirdly Nordic inflections. Art Lester was from Virginia, and explained the Maine weather like one who had known it all his life and known Maine all his life. When we parodied his voice, we spoke in exaggerated Down East accents, never realizing that this most authentic of voices we imitated was a southern one. A friend from San Francisco still bursts out with "a turn toward the inclement" on occasion, with a contrived accent and loud laugh, recalling a visit to Maine, and the day he heard Art Lester use that then-singular expression.

Art Lester died today, drowned on Sebago.

I have had one dog in my life, a hippie dog of a hippie owner, I would say, a dog who was never fixed because it would have been somehow unnatural. He was medium-sized, never much on the leash, and spent most of his second year of life in dogfights, losing them all. He was named Atrocites, pronounced as if a Greek hero in Homer, because one drunken night years before I owned him, a friend and I joked of such names: Atrocites, the Greek general known for his war crimes; Erogenus, the Roman emperor known for his orgies. Or maybe all these names were just told to me that night. In any case, "Big A," a bulldog as he became to be, was born before his time. Some neighbor, the wife of a Navy man I suppose, yelled across the street once to keep my damn dog away from her dog because her kids were watching; and I yelled back I couldn't be responsible for her kids not knowing what was natural and if her damn dog was in heat, she had best keep it inside, and she yelled back how goddamn natural did I think it was having my damn dog lick her dog's dick, and finally, hippie and redneck, we both laughed and there was no more trouble. No more trouble until Father took it upon himself to spare me the trouble of killing my dog and took the dog to the vet himself while I drank coffee in the guesthouse. I forgave him for dying, but not for that.

So the dog, Big A, went down today, and Father went down today, and the world did not seem the same. It is the ordinary things—the dogs dying and the fathers dying—that make us feel so extraordinary and singular, left behind.

And Gabor died today. A Hungarian scholar of medieval French could not have found a more alienating way to spend his life than teaching Old French to privileged college kids on the seabound coast of Maine. When I last saw him he was barely conscious from all the Valium. "In these days," he hears me say, "a man needs more than a drafty garage and a smoothly running car." And instead of dying peacefully, he went back to New York for a second round of chemotherapy and maybe a second operation, and there he died in the agony he was trying to spare himself, with Linda Jane, I found out years later, at his side.

And I thought about sailing then and wondered if I had had the narrative powers to help him die as easily as he wanted to die. "He fell overboard," the vessel owner said. "I saw nothing. I could not work my way back to him. I sailed in circles for an hour."

And Linda Jane's dog died today. Linda Jane sent me a rare e-mail and I called her immediately. The dog had grown old in the years I knew Linda Jane, and had spent the last two years aging and stumbling and sleeping and looking up to remind us that the end was inevitable and near. She died today, and all the plans of burying her in the backyard and keeping a tuft of her groomed fur as a memento went awry as the hole filled with water, and the vet came too early, and this is exactly the same story I heard years earlier from Linda Jane in New Mexico who tried the same thing with her beloved D'Artacgnan. The dogs we have loved simply will not die for us, even though we try to help them do that, but finally die for them, maybe looking up in astonishment, or feeling our own stress and anguish and hurling it back to us, or maybe without enough self-consciousness to have any awareness about the consequences of what is happening to them.

And Linda Jane herself died today—slim, and self-medicating—a sports enthusiast who died at thirty, taking with her the foolish unprotecting cross about her neck and the date with me to the hockey game she had canceled a week before. Linda Jane, slim like Linda Jane working the genoa years ago, and now and always dead-at-thirty. She sat at the library desk with her taut profile, slowly weakening, and one day I go to the library and there are only strewn flowers on the desks where I used to look for her.

And John died today as well, taking with him many memories of him and all his memories of me—that day, some forty years ago, driving to New York with Linda Jane to get the motorcycles from Bedford; Linda Jane, beloved of animals, the wild ones that she fed and the dog she kept for me when I left her. That day, now nearly forty years ago, through Hartford and Danbury and towns I had never heard of, as I lay in the back of the old Volvo with Linda Jane beside me, shocked at what I was feeling, shocked that a twenty-two-year-old had not, in fact, experienced all that life was. "What was it that we said?" I wrote. Did it rain on those momentous days?

And David died today from injuries, drunken and blood-spattered, with his leg gone and finally in the terminal care of the doctors and the nurses he despised. And Wes Alexander, too, drowned as fishermen who cannot swim drown, the only one who ever really spoke to us. And Tom Coffin, grand charmer that he was and maybe a bit disreputable as sometimes I think the entire lot of them are or can be and I write of his stilted funeral, "His fishing boat unfinished now for good." And Dick Nesbitt, wounded in Vietnam, his boat finally sailing in circles without him. I try to think of him, so brooding and beautiful. But all I have is an irrelevance from football. He ran in his then-astounding grace, head down, as one should never do, and I, sixteen, saw my chance and nearly knocked him unconscious as others had so often done to me. I should change our roles, I think, paying tribute to him and to his brothers, all better sailors and athletes than I would ever be. But these idiot glories of our childhoods mean too much to us, and I simply cannot do it.

And far less justly, John's son died today, leaving him in grief, and Linda Jane's son drowned too on Sebago before I even knew her, and not a day goes by when I see them that they do not speak of these bad things.

Ashore somewhere, my colleagues died as well and for some, we have come to construct elaborate and lugubrious public services. For others, Jack, whose cruising skills I loved, we have sternly spared not the least of words. And those old teachers died today, Old Scratch himself, as I called him, and Jackson died and perhaps those other teachers too, Arnold Johnson and Marvin Morillo and Leslie Whitbread whom I have forgotten to contact until today. And students die, as I obliquely hear, and I suppose their students die as well, and all of them died today. The family of my wife, and Linda Jane sick with cancer and multitudes of them as I sit here, cold, with another season nearly gone on the water.

And all the others died today. All the parents and grandparents and aunts and uncles—who is to know how many? Father from the cancer that terrified him as he smoked the endless cigarettes, and Mother in the dementia that she most feared as she bit her lip stoically and made up intricate stories to hide the death of her intellect. And Uncle Joe is gone, overcome by the smoking and hacking cough of so many men of his generation, and Frank too who can now be forgiven for all the things I never knew about. And Huck,

I suppose, and Bunny, and others too of that life to which I have too few connections now even to hear news of their passing.

I think of sitting here a year ago with Linda Jane's old dying dog, and maybe when I edit this it will be years ago. Linda Jane is in New York, and the dog breathes heavily, sleeping on the couch. There is one more walk ahead late in the day. One more bowl of Kibbles, I believe they now are called. And then Linda Jane will return and I'll leave Maine for the winter and Linda Jane will have the dog, and I will get one e-mail about all of it this winter. And as I write and revise this now, the dog, as you know too, is gone as well.

I'll drive or I'll be driven to the airport, past the boatyard where my boat is stored for the winter, and I won't glance at the covered hull, since there is nothing I can really do about it all until the spring. The ice forms on the rail and the old and badly varnished teak turns an irritating speckled green that will need to be scraped away next season. And instead of thinking about the real and the important things, I imagine what I could have done to prevent that—taking the time to apply repeated coats correctly, or perhaps using a different formula of varnish, or perhaps letting the woodwork age in peace and dereliction. You must be methodical in varnishing, I think. There is no room for idle hope. Each slightest imperfection must be sanded clear, for each imperfection will burn its way through the covering coats, and instead of sanding one coat away you will scrape two or three or four away and start again. And I think of that, and the mistakes made on the varnishings and the dog's death protect me from the real and the important things once again.

In *Tristram Shandy*, Sterne writes that he can be immortal through constructing his mock autobiography, since the time it takes to write is greater than the time he describes, two years to write of the nine months between his conception and birth. But as I write this, what I experience is not like that at all; the revisions simply increase the number of entries here and the way I must treat them. And as I write, there will be others like A and B and C and those I refuse to name here for fear of condemning both of us to this inevitability.

So Father dies again today, and Mother finally follows him, drugged to get it right one last time in the nursing home, recovering from her last stroke. And now it is time for Linda Jane as well, oblivious to my tribute to her, lying there in her memories with her consort and all her failings with her, inscribed here and in the dedication of the book I sent to her two years ago. It is late evening in the darkness, and I stare at my wife-to-be. Thinking of the sleep I've missed; thinking of my sudden inability to judge what others think of her. Knowing that life will never be the same for me again.

LATE JUNE

Past the solstice, the days no longer lengthen; the kids are now out of school, and the boats from away as they are known begin their slow journey east for the summer, most with serious sailors from Portland or Boston or New York or the Chesapeake, who rarely travel slower than five knots and thus glide past at hull speed with their tuned diesels barely audible and their wakes barely rippling. It is late June and my spring trip, or *mon voyage* as it is known to those I call my West Coast family, is nearly over; I am heading west or about to head west. The air is warm and there is no more need to heat the cabin with candles and the alcohol stove. The ice is gone and the boat smells like whatever was last cooked or died there or was discarded or defecated in the cabin.

The scaled filth on the hull looks like sailing filth—the fine mud from the anchor—but in all likelihood it is not. It is rather the residue of spring blows that rip the pollen from the evergreens; the pollen is driven out to sea in the winds from the west and north and cakes even the most seaward boats in green. I am mildly envious of the large clean boats cruising quietly and competently to the east, with their well-mannered children now free for the summer.

I now think about the contrariness of the good winds from the southwest, the beating against them, and the day-sailing that will more than do for the rest of the summer. I will spend much of the next week listening to Art Lester, or the computers who replaced him on NOAA radio, and calculating in a pointless way the number of days it will take to get home and the time of day and whether I will mow the lawn and what my computer will look like and who my next visitor will be.

On these trips back, I meet Linda Jane in Rockland; she will have systematically packed strawberries from her garden. For her, the uneventful tack out of Rockland Harbor will be heaven. To her, the slow way of the nearly wakeless boat leaving the wharf in the early morning breezes and currents is what, she says, one lives for. She means of course those few days of the earliest summer with everyone free from school and the powerboats launched and the spring bills paid.

Those days require hours of tacking, working against the wind through Mussel Ridge Channel, or rounding Mosquito Island and sailing inland past Port Clyde, where the wind is soft in all conditions; you have to slog through the irritant of seas in light air off Pemaquid, and the tide is likely unpredictable near the Kennebec River and Seguin. Yet despite that, I feel the same ease I feel when imagining some catastrophic injury or disease. The blood pool on the sidewalk expanding as I kneel before it. The nurses. The unnecessary mornings in the emergency room. It is over, I think, smug in the heroics of it all. There will be no more worrying about weather conditions, or failed equipment, or missed appointments. This sense of ease is not about, say, love of the boat or the water or the being alone, but about freedom from the pressure of the forced enjoyment of the season.

Linda Jane is experiencing her first day of near calm. We rest at anchor in Greenland Cove in the fog in Muscongus Bay, and the boat owned by a friend from high school, now a dentist in the area, is moored a few hundred yards to the north. It might be warm enough in that cove to swim this time of year, or at least, as we might say, to give it a shot. From there, it is ten miles straight into the prevailing wind to Pemaquid, but we do not leave until the late afternoon, drift sailing through the light fog into the small harbor of Round Pond. Magical though it once was, the harbor is now clogged with large boats with only a small place to anchor on its outer portion. I realize, anchored there, I will never return, since even this small spot will in a season or two be buried in moorings.

The next morning is clear, and we are able to sail off that anchor at nine, I think, and it is a perfect time to be sailing this section of Muscongus Bay. The tide is ebbing straight out past Pemaquid and will turn at noon. It is an eight-mile run to the bell buoy off Pemaquid, but the knot log registers only half of them in the four hours it takes to barely drift past the lighthouse. A year later we will pass this same spot, and we will neither hear nor see that lighthouse in the fog, but Linda Jane will be talking about this day, this particular day of drifting without the engine, past Pemaquid. It is a day she will claim always to remember as the epitome, she says, of my stubbornness, although to me, of course, it is all quite different. I remember reaching Pemaquid, by contrast, exactly as the tide turned, and steering, insofar as that was possible, north into Johns Bay, wondering if there was another miracle of tide that could take us the four miles to McFarland Cove and Witch Island with barely enough wind to maintain steerage. And every time I sail there I remember a different day I sailed into this bay with Linda Jane, years earlier, and we anchored to the east in the sand of Pemaquid Beach.

We drift in the light air, and at 4 PM we drift past Witch Island, and Linda Jane is most interested in the detail I reveal about wishing for sufficient breeze to get the anchors set. She will tell this tale herself, embellishing it with the detail of the anchors, although I'm not sure she understands the subtleties of my reasonings. Inside Witch Island, the tide runs harder than the wind at night, shifting directions inevitably twice, and for years I have set two anchors here, although even on the worst days all this nautical rigmarole, as Mother might have termed it, is likely unnecessary.

This astonishing day is one Linda Jane will describe in years to come as competing against the seaweed, that is, trying to outsail the flotsam drifting in the current. Amusing though this is, she claims also that never again will we spend eight hours drifting in the currents just because I would prefer, if possible, not to use the engine. In her own boat, modeled after mine, on the last trip we took together, she will announce before we begin that as long as she is in charge, there will be no days like this one, however glorious it may have seemed to me. That we will control our speed and distance and the things that happen to us, and never again will we simply give such matters up to chance. Sailing will be, I remember thinking, sailing efficiently in the southwest breeze with her, like what she herself calls "car sailing," that is, driving up the coast together in the fall, after sailing season, with the well-marked gazetteer, visiting all those places I have seen and she has sometimes seen from the water. It will be like well-planned nights with relatives or the motel in Eastport where the dog got us evicted from a "pet free" room for barking at the owner. This is what sailing will be, and nothing at all as it was when the seaweed seemed to drift past the hull in the dark placid waters of Johns Bay on that June day.

I am sailing alone into Potts Harbor, now home. There is a tangle of buoys that marks a channel easily negotiated, once you are used to it. The tide is running against me, and knowing that channel well does not help when that current is greater than what the knot meter registers as "speed through water." After twenty minutes, I turn on the engine, even though I have avoided this all day. When I motor out of the channel currents and into the quiet basin, I cut the engine, so that I can say I sailed the last half mile to the mooring. Linda Jane is on the wharf. I do not see her clearly, but I recognize the pacings of her inseparable dog. She will tell me later how her heart raced as she saw me in the channel, but she will not see the ignominy of the engine fumes, nor would she care if she had seen them.

The water is quiet. I can think about cars starting and

grass to be mowed, and perhaps there will be a pile of mail or a long list of e-mail I can deal with. I will walk past the marina and perhaps I will feel what I used to call the effects of sea legs. There was a year too I cried on the last leg sailing across Casco Bay. Now, I am lucky if I can clearly remember the feeling.

Linda Jane is on the wharf. Her dog paces in wonderment about her. It is late June and the clean, well-mannered sloops slip noiselessly to the east.

EPILOGUE

You hate me.

—Linda Jane

It is winter and I sit at an empty and mismatched table in a coffee shop in the always-seasonable weather of California. I have ordered espresso, which will likely keep me awake for hours, and I read a postmodern novel written by a friend while Linda Jane sits two tables away in the center of the room on this Sunday night in Los Angeles. I turn a page of the novel but I am not really reading it. Women this young, who see themselves as voluptuous, do not sit innocently in the middle of coffee shops at 9 PM on a Sunday, I think, with their flesh exposed as they write furiously on what seems to be a set of school papers—front, stare, turn the leaf over, write on the back. She holds her pen too tightly and clumsily. I will say: "You are a teacher." "You are grading." "You are a professor." She may be any of these— a high school teacher, a graduate student; perhaps she has a job at a nearby community college. Which one will put her here on a Sunday? If she is a college teacher, her eyes will meet my eyes, but I am not certain that they do. She is on display. But she is not on display for me.

If I say "teacher," meaning public school teacher, and she is instead that imagined graduate student, she will answer me with the condescension my own students reserve for me. If I say "professor," and she is instead that public school teacher, she will be embarrassed and defensive. I pretend to read, as a young man, poorly dressed, bad hair, unhealthy, overweight, makes the advance I calculate. He asks clumsily about a label on her computer. She leans forward and smiles to answer. But this would-be seducer has prepared no second question, I think in derision. He might sit down, I think, and the two of them could then examine the computer screen. But he leaves.

One evening, years ago, I might have said: "You grading? You must be grading?"

But the papers she reads make no such sense to me. Ruled, with diagrams, or illustrations, writing, then her own writing. They are unlike any papers I have ever seen, even though the process of dealing with them seems familiar. What are they, and why is she so intent on them in this so public place?

She looks up at me. She does not know the postmodern novel I am reading is in fact a postmodern novel. She does not know what "postmodern" is or means. She does not know the author is my friend, or that there is not one author for this book but two. She is listening in her earphones to music I cannot hear, and her computer screen is turned away from me. She was lovelier, the fox in Aesop might be thought to think, a year ago or the year before that year.

This final line just never seemed quite right to me. I revise it one year later, sobbing on that last awful flight to LAX from Boston, to the apartment you left empty, as Linda Jane, it seems, across the aisle, grades essays on Herodotus.

~~~

It is November, and I walk in the deserted field behind the wharf where Linda Jane last waited for me. My friends who own this field and its majestic views are gone for the winter. There are no boats but working boats in the water.

Thinking now as clearly as I can this cold November day, I remember my earliest grade reports, saved of course by my mother and stored in a musty cabinet of what is now a summer home. They say I do not play well with other children. They describe me, in this waste of my memory, as either "stout" or "stocky." In those days, not knowing what such language meant, I guessed that most of what one was or did was laudable. I played Maine alone in those days, on the cobblestone beach in Kennebunk or in the artificial pond, that breeding ground of newts, dug out by a neighbor on a road near Brunswick, or in the snow that covered that pond in winter. I didn't need to get the words right. I never imagined I would one day be on the water rather than simply in it, with the mud on my feet and the newly thawed ice on my hands.

There were other fields like this when I was twelve, but I cannot identify them. Thinking now more clearly on this November day, I believe that nothing matters when one is ten or was it twelve; and nothing matters now, although I still don't have the words right. The ponds and the beach at Kennebunk never disappointed me, I'll say, or perhaps they promised nothing. I did not know that this would pass. I would be older. I would be past the days playing on the pond and on the cobblestone beach at Kennebunk. I would outgrow it. I will outgrow it. One day I will have outgrown it. I will live forever.

And then I was a teenager, having outgrown nothing. And suddenly, things mattered, as they did so crucially for decades, with the loved ones dying and all that embarrassment over my mistakes made on the water. The boat high and dry on the ledge now named for me. Overshooting the mooring. Linda Jane laughing. Linda Jane, older and so experienced, laughing in the arms of another. I would live, now I thought, merely to overcome these sad particulars.

Yet I never grew into that second future I imagined, just into that peculiar indifference of one who walks in the field frost or along a cobblestone shore. I say now nothing is crucial or of consequence, whether Linda Jane laughs in the arms of a lover or waits on the wharf for me with her heart all aflutter. And I will not live forever as once I would, as I

walk in those fields behind the last wharf still on the water.
Or so I say.

The working boats catch the evening breeze, and turn in
unison toward the wind.